JESUS
OUR GREAT
HOPE

CRISWELL FREEMAN

THOMAS NELSON
Since 1798

NASHVILLE DALLAS MEXICO CITY RIO DE JANEIRO

Published in Nashville, Tennessee, by Thomas Nelson.

Thomas Nelson titles may be purchased in bulk for educational, business, fund-raising, or sales promotional use. For information, please e-mail SpecialMarkets@ThomasNelson.com.

Unless otherwise noted, Scripture quotations are taken from THE NEW KING JAMES VERSION. © 1982 by Thomas Nelson. Used by permission. All rights reserved. Scripture quotations marked NCV are taken from New Century Version®. © 2005 by Thomas Nelson. Used by permission. All rights reserved. Scripture quotations marked KJV are taken from the King James Version of the Bible. Scripture quotations marked NIV are taken from the Holy Bible, New International Version®, NIV®. Copyright © 1973, 1978, 1984, 2011 by Biblica, Inc.® Used by permission of Zondervan. All rights reserved worldwide. www.zondervan.com

ISBN: 978-0-529-12389-3

Printed in the United States of America

14 15 16 17 18 RRD 6 5 4 3 2 1

Contents

HOPE *for* EVERYDAY LIVING

――― ❧ ―――

I wait for the LORD, my soul waits, and in His word I do hope.
My soul waits for the LORD more than those who watch for the
morning—yes, more than those who watch for the morning.

PSALM 130:5–6

When hope seems to be in short supply, there is a source to which we can turn in order to restore our perspective and our strength. That source is God. When we lift our prayers to the Creator, we avail ourselves of God's power, God's wisdom, and God's love. And when we allow God's Son to reign over our hearts, we are transformed, not just for a day, but for all eternity.

Are you looking for a renewed sense of hope? If so, it's time to place your future in the loving hands of God's only begotten Son. When you do, you'll discover that hope is not only highly perishable but that it is also readily renewable . . . one day—and one moment—at a time.

Like the winds of the sea are the ways of fate as we voyage
through our life. 'Tis the set of the soul that decides the goal
and not the storm or the strife.

~ELLA WHEELER WILCOX

WORSHIP HIM

*For it is written, "You shall worship the LORD
your God, and Him only you shall serve."*

MATTHEW 4:10

The more intently you worship God, the more likely you are to remain a hope-filled believer. When you choose to worship the Father sincerely and often, you reap a plentiful harvest of joy, peace, and abundance. But if you distance yourself from God by foolishly worshiping earthly possessions or personal gratification, you'll be making a mistake of profound proportions.

Have you accepted the grace of God's only begotten Son? Then worship Him. Worship Him today and every day. Worship Him with sincerity and thanksgiving. Write His name on your heart and rest assured that He too has written your name on His.

Worship is about rekindling an ashen heart into a blazing fire.
~LIZ CURTIS HIGGS

In commanding us to glorify Him, God is inviting us to enjoy Him.

~C. S. LEWIS

THE SHEPHERD'S GIFT

My cup runs over. Surely goodness and mercy shall follow me all the days of my life; and I will dwell in the house of the LORD forever.

PSALM 23:5–6

The Word of God is clear: Christ came in order that we might have life abundant and life eternal. Eternal life is a priceless possession of all who invite Christ into their hearts, but God's abundance is optional. He does not force it upon us.

When we entrust our hearts and our days to the One who created us, we experience abundance through the grace and sacrifice of His Son. But when we turn our thoughts and direct our energies away from God's commandments, we inevitably forfeit the spiritual abundance that might otherwise be ours.

Do you sincerely seek the riches that our Savior offers to those who give themselves to Him? Then follow Him completely and obey Him without reservation. When you do, you will receive the love and the abundance that He has promised. Seek first the salvation that is available through a personal relationship with Jesus Christ, and then claim the joy, the peace, and the spiritual abundance that the Shepherd offers His sheep.

People, places, and things were never meant to give us life. God alone is the author of a fulfilling life.

~GARY SMALLEY AND JOHN TRENT

In TIMES *of* ADVERSITY

For whatever is born of God overcomes the world. And this is the victory that has overcome the world—our faith.

1 JOHN 5:4

All of us face times of adversity. On occasion, we all must endure the disappointments and tragedies that befall believers and nonbelievers alike. The reassuring words of 1 John 5:4 remind us that when we accept God's grace, we overcome the passing hardships of this world by relying upon His strength, His love, and His promise of eternal life.

When we call upon God in heartfelt prayer, He will answer—in His own time and according to His own plan—and He will heal us. And while we are waiting for God's plans to unfold and for His healing touch to restore us, we can be comforted in the knowledge that our Creator will and can overcome any obstacle, even if we cannot. Let us take God at His word, let us trust Him, and let us have hope for today, for tomorrow, and for eternity.

> *Adversity is always unexpected and unwelcomed. It is an intruder and a thief, and yet in the hands of God, adversity becomes the means through which His supernatural power is demonstrated.*
>
> ~CHARLES STANLEY

CONTAGIOUS FAITH

Now the just shall live by faith.

HEBREWS 10:38

*H*ope, like enthusiastic Christianity, is contagious. If you enjoy a hope-filled, life-altering relationship with God, that relationship will have an impact on others—perhaps a profound impact.

Are you genuinely excited about your faith and your future? And do you make your enthusiasm known to those around you? Or are you a "silent ambassador" for Christ? God's preference is clear: He intends for you to stand before others and proclaim your faith.

Does Christ reign over your life? If so, then it's time to share your testimony, your hopes, and your enthusiasm. The world needs all three.

Enthusiasm, like the flu, is contagious—we get it from one another.

~BARBARA JOHNSON

There seems to be a chilling fear of holy enthusiasm among the people of God. We try to tell how happy we are—but we remain so well-controlled that there are very few waves of glory experienced in our midst.

~A. W. TOZER

COMPASSIONATE SERVANTS

Finally, all of you be of one mind, having compassion for one another; love as brothers, be tenderhearted, be courteous.

1 PETER 3:8

God's Word commands us to be compassionate, generous servants to those who need our support. As believers, we have been richly blessed by our Creator. We, in turn, are called to share our gifts, our possessions, our testimonies, and our talents.

Concentration camp survivor Corrie ten Boom correctly observed, "The measure of a life is not its duration but its donation." These words remind us that the quality of our lives is determined not by what we are able to take from others, but instead by what we are able to share with others.

The thread of compassion is woven into the very fabric of Christ's teachings. If we are to be disciples of Christ, we too must be zealous in caring for others. Our Savior expects no less from us. And He deserves no less.

Compassion is sometimes the fatal capacity for feeling what it is like to live inside somebody else's skin. It is the knowledge that there can never really be any peace and joy for me until there is peace and joy finally for you too.

~FREDERICK BUECHNER

The Remedy of Uncertainty

—⁓⸲⸲⁓—

But He said to them, "Why are you fearful, O you of little faith?"
Then He arose and rebuked the winds and the sea, and there was a
great calm.

Matthew 8:26

In Matthew 8, we are told of a terrible storm that rose quickly on the Sea of Galilee while Jesus and His disciples were in a boat, far from shore. The disciples were filled with fear.

Sometimes, like Jesus' disciples, we feel threatened by the storms of life. Sometimes we may feel distant from God, and sometimes we may question His power or His plans. During these moments, when our hopes begin to fade and our fears begin to multiply, we must remember that God is not simply near, He is here.

Are you being tested? If so, remember that God is always with you, always willing to calm the storms of life. When you sincerely seek His presence—and when you genuinely seek to establish a deeper, more meaningful relationship with His Son—God is prepared to touch your heart, calm your fears, answer your doubts, and restore your hopes.

Struggling with God over the issues of life doesn't show a lack of faith—that is faith.

~Lee Strobel

Faith That Works

Thus also faith by itself, if it does not have works, is dead.

God stands by your side through every stage of your life, ready to strengthen you and protect you if you have faith in Him. When you place your faith, your trust, indeed your life in the hands of Christ Jesus, you'll be amazed at the marvelous things He can do with you and through you.

So, promise yourself that your faith will be a faith that works. How do you keep that promise to strengthen your faith? Through praise, worship, Bible study, and prayer. These things will help you learn to trust God's plans. With Him, all things are possible, and He stands ready to open a world of possibilities to you if you have faith.

> *Faith is our spiritual oxygen. It not only keeps us alive in God, but enables us to grow stronger.*
> ~Joyce Landorf Heatherly

> *It is faith that saves us, not works, but the faith that saves us always produces works.*
> ~C. H. Spurgeon

A WALK *with* GOD

---❦~❦---

*"For I have given you an example, that you
should do as I have done to you."*

JOHN 13:15

*J*esus Christ is not only our Lord and Savior; He is also the perfect example for how we should live our lives. Every day we are confronted with countless opportunities to follow in the footsteps of Jesus. When we do, our heavenly Father guides our steps and blesses our endeavors. As citizens of a fast-changing world, we face challenges that sometimes leave us feeling overworked, overcommitted, and overwhelmed. But God has different plans for us. He intends that we slow down long enough to praise Him and glorify His Son. When we do, He lifts our spirits and enriches our lives.

Today provides a glorious opportunity to place yourself in the service of the One who is the Giver of all blessings. May you seek His will, may you trust His word, and may you walk in the footsteps of His Son.

The Christian faith is meant to be lived moment by moment. It isn't some broad, general outline—it's a long walk with a real Person. Details count: passing thoughts, small sacrifices, a few encouraging words, little acts of kindness, brief victories over nagging sins.

~JONI EARECKSON TADA

ACCEPTING HIS ABUNDANCE

"Give, and it will be given to you: good measure, pressed down, shaken together, and running over will be put into your bosom. For with the same measure that you use, it will be measured back to you."

LUKE 6:38

The Bible gives us hope that as Christians we can enjoy lives filled with abundance.

But what, exactly, did Jesus mean when, in John 10:10, He promised "life . . . more abundantly"? Was He referring to material possessions or financial wealth? Hardly. Jesus offers a different kind of abundance: a spiritual richness that extends beyond the temporal boundaries of this world.

Is material abundance part of God's plan for our lives? Perhaps. But in every circumstance of life, during times of wealth or times of want, God will provide us what we need if we trust Him (Matthew 6). May we, as believers, claim the riches of Christ Jesus every day that we live, and may we share His blessings with all who cross our path.

God has promised us abundance, peace, and eternal life. These treasures are ours for the asking; all we must do is claim them. One of the great mysteries of life is why on earth do so many of us wait so very long to lay claim to God's gifts?

~MARIE T. FREEMAN

FORGIVENESS IS GOD'S WAY

_Be kind and loving to each other, and forgive each
other just as God forgave you in Christ._

EPHESIANS 4:32 NCV

To forgive others is difficult. Being frail, fallible, imperfect human beings, we are quick to anger, quick to blame, slow to forgive, and even slower to forget. No matter. Forgiveness, no matter how difficult, is God's way, and it must be our way too.

God's commandments are not intended to be customized for the particular whims of particular believers. God's word is not a menu from which each of us may select items à la carte, according to our own desires. Far from it. God's Holy Word is a book that must be taken in its entirety; all of God's commandments are to be taken seriously. And so it is with forgiveness. So if you hold bitterness against even a single person, forgive. Then, to the best of your abilities, forget. It's God's way for you to live.

_Looking back over my life, all I can see is mercy and grace
written in large letters everywhere. May God help me have
the same kind of heart toward those who wound or offend me._
~JIM CYMBALA

Forgiveness is rarely easy, but it is always right.
~CYNTHIA HEALD

ACCEPTING YOURSELF

God began doing a good work in you, and I am sure he will continue it until it is finished when Jesus Christ comes again.

PHILIPPIANS 1:6 NCV

*A*ccepting other people can be difficult. But sometimes we find it even more difficult to accept ourselves.

We have high expectations and lofty goals. We want to achieve them now, not later. And we want our lives to unfold according to our own wishes and our own timetables—not God's.

The Bible affirms the importance of self-acceptance by exhorting believers to love others as they love themselves (Matthew 22:37–40). Furthermore, the Bible teaches that when we genuinely open our hearts to Him, God accepts us just as we are. And if He accepts us—faults and all—then who are we to believe otherwise?

The great freedom Jesus gives us is to be ourselves, defined by His love and our inner qualities and gifts rather than by any kind of show we put on for the world.

~LESLIE WILLIAMS

By the grace of God you are what you are; glory in your self-hood, accept yourself and go on from there.

~WILFERD PETERSON

STRENGTH *for the* DAY

I can do all things through Christ who strengthens me.

PHILIPPIANS 4:13

Have you made God the cornerstone of your life, or is He relegated to a few hours on Sunday morning? Have you genuinely allowed God to reign over every corner of your heart, or have you attempted to place Him in a spiritual compartment? The answer to these questions will determine the direction of your day and your life.

God loves you. In times of trouble, He will comfort you; in times of sorrow, He will dry your tears. When you are weak or sorrowful, God is as near as your next breath. He stands at the door of your heart and waits. Welcome Him in and allow Him to rule. And then accept the peace, strength, protection, and abundance that only God can give.

In my weakness, I have learned, like Moses, to lean hard on God. The weaker I am, the harder I lean on Him. The harder I lean, the stronger I discover Him to be. The stronger I discover God to be, the more resolute I am in this job He's given me to do.

~JONI EARECKSON TADA

COMPASSIONATE CHRISTIANITY

God has chosen you and made you his holy people. He loves you. So you should always clothes yourselves with mercy, kindness, humility, gentleness, and patience.

COLOSSIANS 3:12 NCV

How can you practice compassionate Christianity? By making kindness a centerpiece of your dealings with others.

The instructions of Colossians 3:12 are unambiguous: as Christians, we are to be compassionate, humble, gentle, and kind. But sometimes we fall short. In the busyness and confusion of daily life, we may neglect to share a kind word or a kind deed. This oversight hurts others, but it hurts us most of all.

Today, slow yourself down and be alert for those who need your smile, your kind words, or your helping hand. Today, honor Christ by following and obeying His Golden Rule. He deserves no less, and neither, for that matter, do your friends.

As much as God loves to hear our worship and adoration, surely he delights all the more in seeing our gratitude translated into simple kindnesses that keep the chain of praise unbroken, alive in others' hearts.

~EVELYN CHRISTENSON

The GREATEST *of* THESE

And now abide faith, hope, love, these three;
but the greatest of these is love.

1 CORINTHIANS 13:13

The beautiful words of 1 Corinthians 13 remind us that love is God's commandment. Faith is important, of course. So too is hope. But love is more important still. We are commanded (not advised, not encouraged . . . commanded!) to love one another just as Christ loved us (John 13:34). That's a tall order, but as Christians, we are obligated to follow it.

Christ showed His love for us on the cross, and we are called upon to return Christ's love by sharing it. Today, let us spread Christ's love to families, friends, and even strangers, so that through us, others might come to know Him.

The cross symbolizes a cosmic as well as a historic truth. Love conquers the world, but its victory is not an easy one.

~REINHOLD NEIBUHR

There are only two duties required of us—the love of God and the love of our neighbor, and the surest sign of discovering whether we observe these duties is the love of our neighbor.

~ST. TERESA OF AVILA

WHERE PEACE BEGINS

"I leave you peace; my peace I give you. I do not give it to you as the world does. So don't let your hearts be troubled or afraid."

JOHN 14:27 NCV

*P*eace with God. Peace with self. Peace with others. Do you possess that kind of peace? Have you found the genuine peace that can be yours through Jesus Christ, or are you still rushing after the illusion of "peace and happiness" that the world promises but cannot deliver? The words of John 14:27 remind us that Jesus offers us peace, not as the world gives, but as He alone gives. Our challenge is to accept Christ's peace into our hearts and then, as best we can, to share His peace with our neighbors.

Today, as a gift to yourself, to your family, and to your friends, claim the inner peace that is your spiritual birthright: the peace of Jesus Christ. It is offered freely; it has been paid for in full; it is yours for the asking. So ask. And then share.

> *The better acquainted you become with God, the less tensions you feel and the more peace you possess.*
> ~CHARLES ALLEN

> *Peace is full confidence that God is Who He says He is and that He will keep every promise in His Word.*
> ~DOROTHY HARRISON PENTECOST

GREAT HOPES, SENSIBLE RISKS

"Is anything too hard for the LORD?"

GENESIS 18:14

s we consider the uncertainties of the future, we are confronted with a powerful temptation: to "play it safe." Unwilling to move mountains, we fret over molehills. Unwilling to entertain great hopes for the tomorrow, we focus on the unfairness of the today. Unwilling to trust God completely, we take timid half steps when God intends for us to make giant leaps.

Today, ask God for the courage to step beyond the boundaries of your doubts. Ask Him to guide you to a place where you can realize your full potential—a place where you are freed from the fear of failure. Ask Him to do His part, and promise Him that you will do your part. Don't ask Him to lead you to a "safe" place; ask Him to lead you to the "right" place. And remember: those two places are seldom the same.

> *God is teaching me to become more and more "teachable": To keep evolving. To keep taking the risk of learning something new . . . or unlearning something old and off base.*
>
> ~BETH MOORE

SUFFICIENT *for* YOUR NEEDS

And God is able to make all grace abound toward you,
that you, always having all sufficiency in all things, may
have an abundance for every good work.

2 CORINTHIANS 9:8

*J*t is easy to become overwhelmed by the demands of everyday life, but if you're a faithful follower of the One from Galilee, you need never be overwhelmed. Why? Because God's love is sufficient to meet your needs. Whatever dangers you may face, whatever heartbreaks you must endure, God is with you, and He stands ready to comfort you and to heal you.

The psalmist wrote, "Weeping may endure for a night, but joy comes in the morning" (Psalm 30:5). But when we are suffering, the morning may seem very far away. It is not. God promises that He is "near to those who have a broken heart" (Psalm 34:18).

If you are experiencing the intense pain of a recent loss, or if you are still mourning a loss from long ago, perhaps you are now ready to begin the next stage of your journey with God. If so, be mindful of this fact: the loving heart of God is sufficient to meet any challenge, including yours.

The grace of God is sufficient for all our needs.
~PETER MARSHALL

Faith Versus Fear

"Don't be afraid, because I am your God. I will make you strong and will help you; I will support you with my right hand that saves you."

ISAIAH 41:10 NCV

Although God has guided us through our struggles and troubles many times before, it is easy for us to lose hope whenever we face adversity, uncertainty, or unwelcome changes.

The next time you find yourself facing a fear-provoking situation, remember that the One who calmed the wind and the waves is also your personal Savior. Then ask yourself which is stronger: your faith or your fear. The answer should be obvious. So when the storm clouds form overhead and you find yourself being tossed on the stormy seas of life, remember this: wherever you are, God is there too. And because He cares for you, you are protected.

> *His hand on me is a father's hand, gently guiding and encouraging. His hand lets me know he is with me, so I am not afraid.*
> ~MARY MORRISON SUGGS

> *Courage faces fear and thereby masters it. Cowardice represses fear and is thereby mastered by it.*
> ~MARTIN LUTHER KING, JR.

Believing Makes *a* Difference

*You have not seen Christ, but still you love him. You cannot
see him now, but you believe in him. So you are filled with a
joy that cannot be explained, a joy full of glory. And you are
receiving the goal of your faith—the salvation of your souls.*

1 PETER 1:8–9 NCV

o you weave your beliefs into the very fabric
of your day? If you do, God will honor your
good works, and your good works will honor God.

If you seek to be a responsible believer, you must
realize that it is never enough to hear the instructions
of God; you must also live by them. And it is never
enough to wait idly by while others do God's work here
on earth. You too must act.

Doing God's work is a responsibility that every
Christian (including you) should bear. And when you
do, your loving heavenly Father will reward your efforts
with a bountiful harvest.

*If all things are possible with God, then all things are possible
to him who believes in him.*

~CORRIE TEN BOOM

*Faith is to believe what you do not see; the reward of this faith
is to see what you believe.*

~ST. AUGUSTINE

Too Busy

The plans of hard-working people earn a profit,
but those who act too quickly become poor.

PROVERBS 21:5 NCV

*A*re you one of those believers who is simply too busy for their own good? Has the hectic pace of life robbed you of the peace that might otherwise be yours through Jesus Christ? If so, you're doing a disservice to yourself and your family.

Through His Son, Jesus, God offers you a peace that passes human understanding, but He won't force His peace upon you; in order to experience it, you must slow down long enough to sense His presence and His love.

Today, take the time to spend some quiet moments with your heavenly Father and let His peace soothe and restore your spirit.

> *It's ironic that one of the best remedies for impending burnout is to give yourself away—to pick out one time and place each week where you can stretch out your hands for the pure joy of doing it.*
>
> ~LIZ CURTIS HIGGS

> *We often become mentally and spiritually barren because we're so busy.*
>
> ~FRANKLIN GRAHAM

Infinite Love

For I am persuaded that neither death nor life, nor angels nor
principalities nor powers, nor things present nor things to come,
nor height nor depth, nor any other created thing, shall be able to
separate us from the love of God which is in Christ Jesus our Lord.

ROMANS 8:38–39

Christ's love for you is both intimate and personal. He gave His life so that you might have the gift of eternal life. His love is unbounded by time or circumstance.

Are you willing to experience an intimate relationship with Jesus? Your Savior is waiting patiently; don't make Him wait a single minute longer. Embrace His love today.

> Christ is like a river that is continually flowing. There are always fresh supplies of water coming from the fountainhead, so that a man may live by it and be supplied with water all his life. So Christ is an ever-flowing fountain; he is continually supplying his people, and the fountain is not spent. They who live upon Christ may have fresh supplies from him for all eternity; they may have an increase of blessedness that is new, and new still, and which never will come to an end.
>
> ~JONATHAN EDWARDS

DURING DARK DAYS

*"I have heard your prayer, I have seen your tears;
surely I will heal you."*

2 KINGS 20:5

The sadness that accompanies any significant loss is an inevitable fact of life. In time, sadness runs its course and gradually abates. Depression, on the other hand, is a physical and emotional condition that does not go away with time. If you find yourself feeling "blue," perhaps it's a logical reaction to the ups and downs of daily life. But if you or someone close to you has become dangerously depressed, it's time to seek a professional evaluation.

Some days are light and happy, and some days are not. When we face the inevitable dark days of life, we must choose how we will respond. Will we allow ourselves to sink even more deeply into our own sadness, or will we do the difficult work of pulling ourselves out? We bring light to the dark days of life by turning first to God, and then to trusted family members, friends, and health professionals. When we do, the clouds will eventually part, and the sun will shine once more upon our souls.

What the devil loves is that vague cloud of unspecified guilt feeling or unspecified virtue by which he lures us into despair.

~C. S. LEWIS

The POWER of
ENCOURAGING WORDS

When you talk, do not say harmful things, but say what people need—words that will help others become stronger. Then what you say will do good to those who listen to you.

EPHESIANS 4:29 NCV

God's Word is filled with illustrations and admonitions concerning the power of the words we speak. Our words have the power to do great good or great harm. If we offer words of encouragement and hope, we can lift others up. And that's precisely what God commands us to do.

Sometimes, when we feel uplifted and secure, it is easy to speak kind words. Other times, when we are discouraged or tired, we can scarcely summon the energy to uplift ourselves, much less anyone else. God intends that we speak words of kindness, wisdom, and truth, no matter our circumstances, no matter our emotions. When we do, we share a priceless gift with the world, and we give glory to the One who gave His life for us. As believers, we must do no less.

The truest help we can render an afflicted man is not to take his burden from him, but to call out his best energy, that he may be able to bear the burden himself.

~PHILLIPS BROOKS

FAITH THAT MOVES MOUNTAINS

"I tell you the truth, you can say to this mountain, 'Go, fall into the sea.' And if you have no doubts in your mind and believe that what you say will happen, God will do it for you."

MARK 11:23 NCV

ecause we live in a demanding world, all of us have mountains to climb and mountains to move. Moving those mountains requires faith.

Are you a mountain mover whose faith is evident for all to see? Hopefully so. God needs more men and women who are willing to move mountains for His glory and for His kingdom.

God walks with you, ready and willing to strengthen you. Accept His strength today. And remember: Jesus taught His disciples that if they had faith, they could move mountains. You can too. So with no further ado, let the mountain moving begin.

Only God can move mountains, but faith and prayer can move God.

~E. M. BOUNDS

God never calls without enabling us. In other words, if he calls you to do something, he makes it possible for you to do it.

~LUCI SWINDOLL

In God We Trust

*And my God shall supply all your need according
to His riches in glory by Christ Jesus.*

PHILIPPIANS 4:19

Countless books have been written about money—how to make it and how to keep it. But if you're a Christian, you probably already own at least one copy—and probably several copies—of the world's foremost guide to financial security. That book is the Holy Bible. God's Word is not only a roadmap to eternal life, it is also an indispensable guidebook for life here on earth. As such, the Bible has much to say about your life, your faith, and your finances.

If you're in need of a financial makeover, God's Word can help. In fact, biblical principles can help you organize your financial life in such a way that you have less need to worry and more time to celebrate God's glorious creation. If that sounds appealing, open your Bible, read its instructions, and follow them.

Here's a good recipe for managing your money: Never make a big financial decision without first talking it over with God.
~MARIE T. FREEMAN

LOVE THAT FORGIVES

"And whenever you stand praying, if you have
anything against anyone, forgive him, that your Father
in heaven may also forgive you your trespasses."

MARK 11:25

Genuine love is an exercise in forgiveness. If we wish to build lasting relationships, we must learn how to forgive. Why? Because our loved ones are imperfect—as are we. How often must we forgive our family and friends? More times than we can count. Why? Because that's what God wants us to do.

Perhaps granting forgiveness is hard for you. If so, you are not alone. Genuine, lasting forgiveness is often difficult to achieve—difficult but not impossible. Thankfully, with God's help, all things are possible, and that includes forgiveness. But even though God is willing to help, He expects you to do some of the work. And make no mistake: forgiveness is work, which is okay with God. He knows that the payoffs are worth the effort.

We pardon to the degree that we love.
~FRANÇOIS DE LA ROCHEFOUCAULD

God expects us to forgive others as He has forgiven us; we are
to follow His example by having a forgiving heart.
~VONETTE BRIGHT

The SEEDS *of* GENEROSITY

"Freely you have received, freely give."

MATTHEW 10:8

When we sow the seeds of generosity, we reap bountiful rewards in accordance with God's plan for our lives. Thus, we are instructed to give cheerfully and without reservation: "But this I say: He who sows sparingly will also reap sparingly, and he who sows bountifully will also reap bountifully. So let each one give as he purposes in his heart, not grudgingly or of necessity; for God loves a cheerful giver" (2 Corinthians 9:6–7).

Today, make this pledge and keep it: I will be a cheerful, generous, courageous giver. The world needs your help, and you need the spiritual rewards that will be yours when you give it.

> *All the blessings we enjoy are divine deposits, committed to our trust on this condition: that they should be dispensed for the benefit of our neighbors.*
>
> ~JOHN CALVIN

> *When somebody needs a helping hand, he doesn't need it tomorrow or the next day. He needs it now, and that's exactly when you should offer to help. Good deeds, if they are really good, happen sooner rather than later.*
>
> ~MARIE T. FREEMAN

Finding Hope

"These things I have spoken to you, that in Me you may have peace. In the world you will have tribulation; but be of good cheer, I have overcome the world."

John 16:33

here are few sadder sights on earth than the sight of a person who has lost all hope. In difficult times, hope can be elusive, but Christians need never lose it. After all, God is good, His love endures, and He has promised His children the gift of eternal life.

If you find yourself falling into the spiritual traps of worry and discouragement, consider the words of Jesus. It was Christ who promised, "In the world you will have tribulation; but be of good cheer, I have overcome the world." This world is indeed a place of trials and tribulations, but as believers, we are secure. God has promised us peace, joy, and eternal life. And God always keeps His promises.

And still today, when you boil it all down, our message to the world—even to the world that comes disguised as our child's schoolteacher, our next-door neighbor, or our personal hair stylist—is hope. Hope beyond the slavery of sin. And hope beyond the grave.

~Becky Tirabassi

A POSITIVE INFLUENCE

*Be an example to the believers in word, in conduct,
in love, in spirit, in faith, in purity.*

1 TIMOTHY 4:12

*A*s followers of Christ, we must each ask ourselves an important question: "What kind
of example am I?" The answer to that question determines, in large part, whether we are positive influences
on our own little corners of the world.

Phillips Brooks advised, "Be such a man, and live
such a life, that if every man were such as you, and
every life a life like yours, this earth would be God's
Paradise." And that's sound advice for men and women
alike because our families and friends are watching . . .
and so, for that matter, is God.

> *If you want your neighbor to know what Christ will do for
> him, let the neighbor see what Christ has done for you.*
> ~HENRY WARD BEECHER

> *Let us preach you, Dear Jesus, without preaching, not by
> words but by our example, by the casting force, the sympa-
> thetic influence of what we do, the evident fullness of the love
> our hearts bear to you. Amen.*
>
> ~MOTHER TERESA

CONDUCT *and* CHARACTER

Lead a quiet and peaceable life in all godliness and reverence.
1 TIMOTHY 2:2

As believers in Christ, we must seek to live each day with discipline, honesty, and faith. When we do, at least two things happen: integrity becomes a habit, and God blesses us because of our obedience to Him.

Living a life of integrity isn't always the easiest way, but it is always the right way . . . and God clearly intends that it should be our way too. Charles Stanley said, "The Bible teaches that we are accountable to one another for our conduct and character."

Character is forged on the anvil of honorable work and polished by the twin virtues of honesty and fairness. Character is a precious thing—difficult to build and wonderful to behold.

Often, our character is at greater risk in prosperity than in adversity.
~BETH MOORE

What lessons about honor did you learn from your childhood? Are you living what you learned today?
~DENNIS SWANBERG

Praise Him

Praise the LORD! Oh, give thanks to the LORD, for
He is good! For His mercy endures forever.

PSALM 106:1

God has blessed us immeasurably, and we owe Him our everlasting praise. Yet sometimes, in our rush to get things done, we simply don't stop long enough to pause and thank our Creator for the countless blessings He has bestowed upon us.

When we slow down and express our gratitude to the One who made us, we enrich our own lives and the lives of those around us. Thus, thanksgiving should become a habit, a regular part of our daily routines. God has blessed us beyond measure, and we owe Him everything, including our never-ending praise. Let us praise Him today, tomorrow, and throughout eternity.

Maintaining a focus on God will take our praise to heights that nothing else can.

~JEFF WALLING

Praise Him! Praise Him! Tell of His excellent greatness.

Praise Him! Praise Him! Ever in joyful song!

~FANNY CROSBY

A QUIET PLACE

Now in the morning, having risen a long while before daylight, He went out and departed to a solitary place; and there He prayed.

MARK 1:35

In the first chapter of Mark, we read that in the darkness of the early-morning hours, Jesus went to a solitary place and prayed. So, too, should we. But sometimes finding quiet moments of solitude is difficult indeed. We live in a noisy world, a world filled with distractions, frustrations, and complications. But if we allow the distractions of a clamorous world to separate us from God's peace, we do ourselves a profound disservice.

Are you one of those busy people who rush through the day with scarcely a single moment for quiet contemplation and prayer? If so, it's time to reorder your priorities. Nothing is more important than the time you spend with your Savior. So be still and claim the inner peace that is your spiritual birthright: the peace of Jesus Christ.

> *We Christians must simplify our lives or lose untold treasures on earth and in eternity. Modern civilization is so complex as to make the devotional life all but impossible. The need for solitude and quietness was never greater than it is today.*
>
> ~A. W. TOZER

WALKING *with* GOD

"Come to Me, all you who labor and are heavy laden, and I will give you rest. Take My yoke upon you and learn from Me, for I am gentle and lowly in heart, and you will find rest for your souls. For My yoke is easy and My burden is light."

MATTHEW 11:28–30

Are you tired? Discouraged? Fearful? Be comforted. Take a walk with God. Jesus called upon believers to walk with Him, and He promised them that He would teach them how to live freely and lightly (Matthew 11:28–30).

Are you worried or anxious? Be confident in God's power. He will never desert you. Do you see no hope for the future? Be courageous and call upon God. He will protect you and then use you according to His purposes. Are you grieving? Know that God hears your suffering. He will comfort you, and in time, He will dry your tears. Are you confused? Listen to the quiet voice of your heavenly Father. He is not a God of confusion. Talk with Him; listen to Him; follow His commandments. He is steadfast, and He is your Protector . . . forever.

As a child of God, rest in the knowledge that your Savior precedes you, and He will walk with you through each experience of your life.

~HENRY BLACKABY

Choosing *the* Good Life

*"And in that day you will ask Me nothing. Most assuredly, I
say to you, whatever you ask the Father in My name He will
give you. Until now you have asked nothing in My name.
Ask, and you will receive, that your joy may be full."*

JOHN 16:23–24

God offers us abundance through His Son, Jesus.
Whether we accept God's abundance is up to
each of us. When we entrust our hearts and our days
to the One who created us, we experience abundance
through the grace and sacrifice of His Son, Jesus. But
when we turn our thoughts and our energies away
from God's commandments, we inevitably forfeit the
spiritual abundance that might otherwise be ours.

What is your focus today? Are you focused on God's
Word and His will for your life? Or are you focused
on the distractions and temptations of a difficult word?
If you sincerely seek the spiritual abundance that your
Savior offers, then follow Him completely and without
reservation. When you do, you will receive the love,
life, and abundance that He has promised.

*The gift of God is eternal life, spiritual life, abundant life
through faith in Jesus Christ, the Living Word of God.*

~ANNE GRAHAM LOTZ

BEYOND ADDICTION

Therefore submit to God. Resist the devil and he will flee from you.
Draw near to God and He will draw near to you. Cleanse your
hands, you sinners; and purify your hearts, you double-minded.

JAMES 4:7–8

nless you're living on a deserted island, you know people who are full-blown addicts—probably lots of people. The dictionary defines *addiction* as "the compulsive need for a habit-forming substance; the condition of being habitually and compulsively occupied with something." That definition is accurate, but incomplete. For Christians, addiction has an additional meaning; it means compulsively worshiping something other than God.

If you, or someone you love, is suffering from the blight of addiction, remember this: help is available. And if you're one of those fortunate people who has never experimented with addictive substances, congratulations. You have just have spared yourself a lifetime of headaches and heartaches.

We are meant to be addicted to God, but we develop secondary
additions that temporarily appear to fix our problems.
~EDWARD M. BERCKMAN

The WISDOM *to* CELEBRATE

A happy heart is like a continual feast.
PROVERBS 15:15 NCV

What will be your attitude today? Will you be fearful, angry, bored, or worried? Will you be cynical, bitter or pessimistic? If so, God wants to have a little talk with you.

The Christian life is a cause for celebration, but sometimes we don't feel much like celebrating. In fact, when the weight of the world seems to bear down upon our shoulders, celebration may be the last thing on our minds, but it shouldn't be. As God's children, we are all blessed beyond measure on good days and bad. This day is a non-renewable resource—once it's gone, it's gone forever.

God created you in His own image, and He wants you to experience hope and abundance. So today, and every day thereafter, celebrate the life that God has given you. Give thanks to the One who has given you everything, and trust in your heart that He wants to give you so much more.

> *You've heard the saying, "Life is what you make it." That means we have a choice. We can choose to have a life full of frustration and fear, but we can just as easily choose one of joy and contentment.*
>
> ~DENNIS SWANBERG

His Intimate Love

"As the Father loved Me, I also have loved you; abide in My love."

JOHN 15:9

illy Graham observed, "God loves you and wants you to experience peace and life—abundant and eternal." Do you believe those words? Do you seek an intimate, one-on-one relationship with your heavenly Father, or are you satisfied to keep Him at a "safe" distance?

Sometimes, in the crush of our daily duties, God may seem far away, but He is not. God is everywhere we have ever been and everywhere we will ever go. He is with us night and day; He knows our thoughts and our prayers. And when we earnestly seek Him, we will find Him because He is here, waiting patiently for us to reach out to Him. May we reach out to Him today and always. And may we praise Him for the glorious gifts that have transformed us today and forever.

Life in God is a great big hug that lasts forever!

~BARBARA JOHNSON

God does not love us because we are valuable. We are valuable because God loves us.

~FULTON J. SHEEN

God's Assurances *and* Your Confidence

"These things I have spoken to you, that in Me you may have peace. In the world you will have tribulation; but be of good cheer, I have overcome the world."

JOHN 16:33

re you a confident believer, or do you live under a cloud of uncertainty and doubt? As a Christian, you have many reasons to be confident. After all, God is in His heaven, Christ has risen, and you are the recipient of God's grace. Despite these blessings, you may, from time to time, find yourself being tormented by negative emotions—and you are certainly not alone.

Even the most faithful Christians are overcome by occasional bouts of fear and doubt. You are no different.

But even when you feel very distant from God, remember that God is never distant from you. When you sincerely seek His presence, He will touch your heart, calm your fears, and restore your confidence.

As I have grown in faith and confidence, I have known more and more that my worth is based on the love of God.
~LESLIE WILLIAMS

COURAGE *for the* STORMS *of* LIFE

But Jesus quickly spoke to them, "Have
courage! It is I. Do not be afraid."

MATTHEW 14:27 NCV

Sometimes we feel threatened by the inevitable storms of life. And when we are fearful, we can turn to Jesus for courage and for comfort.

When a storm rose quickly on the Sea of Galilee, Christ's disciples were afraid. Although they had seen Jesus perform many miracles, the disciples feared for their lives, so they turned to their Savior, and He calmed the waters and the wind.

The next time you're afraid, remember that Jesus can calm the winds and the waves of your own personal storms. That means that you, as a believer whose salvation has already been purchased on the hill at Calvary, can live courageously . . . and you should.

> Down through the centuries, in times of trouble and trial, God has brought courage to the hearts of those who love Him. The Bible is filled with assurances of God's help and comfort in every kind of trouble.
>
> ~BILLY GRAHAM

> What is courage? It is the ability to be strong in trust, in conviction, in obedience. To be courageous is to step out in faith—to trust and obey, no matter what.
>
> ~KAY ARTHUR

The WISDOM *to* BE HUMBLE

When you do things, do not let selfishness or pride be your guide.
Instead, be humble and give more honor to others than to yourselves.
PHILIPPIANS 2:3 NCV

God's Word clearly instructs us to be humble.
And that's good because, as fallible human
beings, we have so very much to be humble about! Yet
some of us continue to puff ourselves up, seeming to
say, "Look at me!" To do so is wrong.

As Christians, we have been refashioned and saved
by Jesus Christ, and that salvation came not because of
our own good works but because of God's grace. How
then can we be prideful? The answer is that if we are
honest with ourselves and with our God, we simply
can't be boastful. We must instead be eternally grateful
and exceedingly humble. The good things in our lives,
including our loved ones, come from God. He deserves
the credit—and we deserve the glorious experience of
giving it to Him.

I have learned that the more we understand how very much
God loves us, and the more we comprehend the grace He has
demonstrated toward us, the more humble we become.
~SERITA ANN JAKES

An Awesome God

The fear of the LORD is a fountain of life.

PROVERBS 14:27

God's hand shapes the universe, and it shapes our lives. God maintains absolute sovereignty over His creation, and His power is beyond comprehension. As believers, we must cultivate a sincere respect for God's awesome power. God has dominion over all things, and until we acknowledge His sovereignty, we lack the humility we need to live righteously, and we lack the humility we need to become wise.

The fear of the Lord is, indeed, the beginning of knowledge. So today, as you face the realities of everyday life, remember this: until you acquire a healthy, respectful fear of God's power, your education is incomplete, and so is your faith.

> *When true believers are awed by the greatness of God and by the privilege of becoming His children, then they become sincerely motivated, effective evangelists.*
>
> ~BILL HYBELS

> *Spiritual worship comes from our very core and is fueled by an awesome reverence and desire for God.*
>
> ~BETH MOORE

Forgiving *and* Forgetting

But the wisdom that is from above is first pure, then peaceable, gentle, willing to yield, full of mercy and good fruits, without partiality and without hypocrisy.

James 3:17

*D*o you have a tough time forgiving and forgetting? If so, welcome to the club. Most of us find it difficult to forgive the people who have hurt us. And that's too bad because life would be much simpler if we could forgive people once and for all and be done with it. Yet forgiveness is seldom that easy. Usually, the decision to forgive is straightforward, but the process of forgiving is more difficult. Forgiveness is a journey that requires time, perseverance, and prayer.

If you sincerely wish to forgive someone, pray for that person. And then pray for yourself by asking God to heal your heart. Don't expect forgiveness to be easy or quick, but rest assured: with God as your partner, you can forgive . . . and you will.

> *Forgiveness does not mean the perpetrator goes free; it means that the forgiver is free and that God will justly deal with those who have caused pain.*
>
> ~Cynthia Heald

> *There is no use in talking as if forgiveness were easy. . . . For we find that the work of forgiveness has to be done over and over again.*
>
> ~C. S. Lewis

OFFERING THANKS

*In everything give thanks; for this is the
will of God in Christ Jesus for you.*

1 THESSALONIANS 5:18

*L*ife has a way of constantly coming at us. Days, hours, and moments are filled with urgent demands requiring our immediate attention.

When the demands of life leave us rushing from place to place with scarcely a moment to spare, we may fail to pause and thank our Creator for His gifts. But whenever we neglect to give proper thanks to the Father, we suffer because of our misplaced priorities.

Today, make a special effort to give thanks to the Creator for His blessings. His love for you is eternal, as are His gifts. And it's never too soon—or too late—to offer Him thanks.

The joy of God is experienced as I love, trust, and obey God— no matter the circumstances—and as I allow Him to do in and through me whatever He wishes, thanking Him that in every pain there is pleasure, in every suffering there is satis- faction, in every aching there is comfort, in every sense of loss there is the surety of the Savior's presence, and in every tear there is the glistening eye of God.

~BILL BRIGHT

Your Talents, His Calling

But as God has distributed to each one, as the Lord has called each one, so let him walk.

1 Corinthians 7:17

*E*very believer has an assortment of gifts and talents. In John 15:16, Jesus said, "You did not choose Me, but I chose you and appointed you that you should go and bear fruit, and that your fruit should remain, that whatever you ask the Father in My name He may give you."

It is terribly important that you heed God's calling by discovering and developing your talents and your spiritual gifts. If you seek to make a difference—and if you seek to bear eternal fruit—you must discover your gifts and begin using them for the glory of God.

Have you found your special calling? If not, keep searching and keep praying until you find it. God has important work for you to do, and the time to begin that work is now.

We can all humbly say in the sincerity of faith, "I am loved; I am called; I am secure."

~Franklin Graham

God has given you special talents—now it's your turn to give them back to God.

~Marie T. Freeman

51

Beyond Guilt

*There is therefore now no condemnation to those
who are in Christ Jesus, who do not walk according
to the flesh, but according to the Spirit.*

ROMANS 8:1

All of us have sinned. Sometimes our sins result from our own stubborn rebellion against God's commandments. And sometimes we are swept up in events that are beyond our abilities to control. Under either set of circumstances, we may experience intense feelings of guilt. But God has an answer for the guilt that we feel. That answer is His forgiveness. When we confess our wrongdoings and repent from them, we are forgiven by the One who created us.

Are you troubled by feelings of guilt or regret? If so, you must repent from your misdeeds, and you must ask your heavenly Father for His forgiveness. When you do, He will forgive you completely and without reservation. Then you must forgive yourself just as God has forgiven you: thoroughly and unconditionally.

You never lose the love of God. Guilt is the warning that temporarily you are out of touch.

~JACK DOMINIAN

The WORLD'S BEST FRIEND

Who's the best friend this world has ever had? Jesus, of course. And when you form a life-changing relationship with Him, He'll will be your best friend too . . . your friend forever.

Jesus has offered to share the gifts of everlasting life and everlasting love with the world and with you. If you make mistakes, He'll stand by you. If you fall short of His commandments, He'll still love you. If you feel lonely or worried, He can touch your heart and lift your spirits.

Jesus wants you to enjoy a happy, healthy, abundant life. He wants you to walk with Him and to share His good news. You can do it. And with a friend like Jesus, you will.

*The dearest friend on earth is but a mere shadow compared
with Jesus Christ.*

~OSWALD CHAMBERS

*When we are in a situation where Jesus is all we have, we soon
discover he is all we really need.*

~GIGI GRAHAM TCHIVIDJIAN

New Beginnings

"I will give you a new heart and put a new spirit within you."

EZEKIEL 36:26

*J*f we sincerely want to change ourselves for the better, we must start on the inside and work our way out from there. Lasting change doesn't occur "out there"; it occurs "in here." It occurs not in the shifting sands of our own particular circumstances, but in quiet depths of our own hearts.

Are you in search of a new beginning or, for that matter, a new you? If so, don't expect changing circumstances to miraculously transform you into the person you want to become. Transformation starts with God, and it starts in the silent center of a humble human heart—like yours.

> *In those desperate times when we feel like we don't have an ounce of strength, He will gently pick up our heads so that our eyes can behold something—something that will keep His hope alive in us.*
>
> ~KATHY TROCCOLI

> *No matter how badly we have failed, we can always get up and begin again. Our God is the God of new beginnings.*
>
> ~WARREN WIERSBE

The IMPORTANCE *of* PRAYER

Be anxious for nothing, but in everything by prayer and supplication, with thanksgiving, let your requests be made known to God.

PHILIPPIANS 4:6

*P*rayer is a powerful tool for communicating with our Creator; it is an opportunity to commune with the Giver of all things good. Prayer is not a thing to be taken lightly or to be used infrequently. Prayer should never be reserved for mealtimes or for bedtimes; it should be an ever-present focus in our daily lives.

In his first letter to the Thessalonians, Paul wrote, "Rejoice evermore. Pray without ceasing. In every thing give thanks: for this is the will of God in Christ Jesus concerning you" (v. 5:17–18 KJV). Paul's words apply to every Christian of every generation. So let us pray constantly about things great and small. God is listening, and He wants to hear from us. Now.

> *We must pray literally without ceasing, in every occurrence and employment of our lives. You know I mean that prayer of the heart which is independent of place or situation, or which is, rather, a habit of lifting up the heart to God, as in a constant communication with Him.*
>
> ~ELIZABETH ANN SETON

TOO WISE *to* BE JEALOUS

If you are selfish and have bitter jealousy in your hearts, do not brag. Your bragging is a lie that hides the truth.

JAMES 3:14 NCV

Are you too wise to be consumed with feelings of jealousy? Hopefully so. After all, Jesus clearly taught us to love our neighbors, not to envy them. But sometimes, despite our best intentions, we fall prey to feelings of resentfulness, jealousy, bitterness, and envy. Why? Because we are human, and because we live in a world that places great importance on material possessions (possessions that, by the way, are totally unimportant to God).

The next time you feel pangs of envy invading your thoughts, remind yourself of two things: (1) envy is a sin, and (2) God has already showered you with so many blessings that if you're a thoughtful, thankful believer, you have no right to ever be envious of any other person on earth.

The jealous are troublesome to others, but a torment to themselves.

~WILLIAM PENN

On the highway of life, envy is an emotional dead end.

~ANONYMOUS

WALK *in* TRUTH

"But when the Spirit of truth comes, he will lead you into all truth."
JOHN 16:13 NCV

The familiar words of John 8:32 remind us that "you shall know the truth, and the truth shall make you free." And St. Augustine had this advice: "Let everything perish! Dismiss these empty vanities! And let us take up the search for the truth."

God is vitally concerned with truth. His Word teaches the truth, His Spirit reveals the truth, and His Son leads us to the truth. When we open our hearts to God, and when we allow His Son to rule over our thoughts and our lives, God reveals Himself, and we come to understand the truth about ourselves and the Truth about God's gift of grace.

Are you seeking the truth and living by it? Hopefully so. When you do, you'll discover that the truth will indeed set you free, now and forever.

Truth will triumph. The Father of truth will win, and the followers of truth will be saved.

~MAX LUCADO

Those who walk in truth walk in liberty.

~BETH MOORE

Thy Will Be Done

"Shouldn't I drink the cup the Father gave me?"

John 18:11 NCV

All of us must, from time to time, endure days filled with suffering and pain. And as human beings with limited understanding, we can never fully understand the plans of our Father in heaven. But as believers in a benevolent God, we must always trust Him.

When Jesus went to the Mount of Olives, He poured out His heart to God (Luke 22). Jesus knew of the agony that He was destined to endure, but He also knew that God's will must be done.

When we face circumstances that shake us to the depths of our souls, we, like Christ, must seek God's will, not our own. When we learn to accept God's will without reservation, we will, in time, come to experience the peace that the Father offers to wise believers (like you) who trust Him completely.

> *The will of God for your life is simply that you submit yourself to Him each day and say, "Father, Your will for today is mine. Your pleasure for today is mine. Your work for today is mine. I trust You to be God. You lead me today and I will follow."*
>
> ~Kay Arthur

HE HEALS

*"I have heard your prayer, I have seen your tears;
surely I will heal you."*

2 KINGS 20:5

Jesus overcame the world, and He promised that we can overcome it too. But sometimes we really don't feel strong enough to overcome anything. Sometimes we experience life-changing personal losses that leave us felling downhearted, discouraged, or worse. When we do, we should remember Christ's assurances, and we should remember that God stands ready to protect us. When we are deeply troubled, we must call upon God, and then, in His own time and according to His own plan, He will heal us.

Are you anxious? Take those anxieties to God. Are you troubled? Take your troubles to Him. Does your world seem to be trembling beneath your feet? Seek protection from the One who cannot be moved. The same God who created the universe will protect you if you ask Him . . . so ask Him.

> *Looking back, my wife Jan and I have learned that the wilderness is part of the landscape of faith, and every bit as essential as the mountaintop. On the mountaintop, we are overwhelmed by God's presence. In the wilderness, we are overwhelmed by his absence. Both places should bring us to our knees; the one, in utter awe; the other, in utter dependence.*
>
> ~DAVE DRAVECKY

REJOICE!

Rejoice in the Lord always. Again I will say, rejoice!

PHILIPPIANS 4:4

Today, celebrate life as God intended. Today, share the good news of Jesus Christ. Today, let us put smiles on our faces, kind words on our lips, and songs in our hearts. Let us be generous with our praise and free with our encouragement.

Oswald Chambers correctly observed, "Joy is the great note all throughout the Bible." However, even the most devoted follower of Jesus occasionally fails to remember that each day should be celebrated for what it is—a gift from God that is beyond measure, that carries no price!

Let us celebrate life to the fullest and invite others to do likewise. After all, God gives very clear instructions for each day's use. He commands us to rejoice and be glad. So, without further hesitation or delay, let the celebration begin!

> *If you can forgive the person you were, accept the person you are, and believe in the person you will become, you are headed for joy. So celebrate your life.*
>
> ~BARBARA JOHNSON

> *I know nothing, except what everyone knows—if there where God dances, I should dance.*
>
> ~W. H. AUDEN

The GIFT of CHEERFULNESS

Worry is a heavy load, but a kind word cheers you up.

PROVERBS 12:25 NCV

Cheerfulness is a gift that we give to others and to ourselves. As believers who have been saved by a risen Christ, why shouldn't we be cheerful? The answer is that we have every reason to honor our Savior with joy in our hearts, smiles on our faces, and words of celebration on our lips.

Christ promises us lives of abundance and joy if we accept His love and His grace. Yet sometimes even the most righteous among us are beset by fits of ill temper and frustration. During these moments, we may not feel like turning our thoughts and prayers to Christ, but that's precisely what we should do. When we do, we simply can't stay grumpy for long.

Cheerfulness prepares a glorious mind for all the noblest acts of religion—love, adoration, praise, and every union with our God.

~St. Elizabeth Ann Seton

Make each day useful and cheerful and prove that you know the worth of time by employing it well. Then youth will be happy, old age without regret, and life a beautiful success.

~Louisa May Alcott

CONTENTMENT THAT LASTS

Serving God does make us very rich, if we are satisfied with what we have. We brought nothing into the world, so we can take nothing out. But, if we have food and clothes, we will be satisfied with that.

1 TIMOTHY 6:6–8 NCV

The preoccupation with happiness and contentment is an ever-present theme in our modern world. We are bombarded with messages that tell us where to find peace and pleasure in a world that worships materialism and wealth.

The world promises to give us contentment through worldly means: wealth, fame, power, and status. But the world is wrong—material possessions and social standing have precious little to do with lasting happiness.

Genuine contentment is a spiritual gift from God to those who trust in Him and follow His commandments. When God dwells at the center of our lives, peace and contentment will belong to us just as surely as we belong to God.

If I could just hang in there, being faithful to my own tasks, God would make me joyful and content. The responsibility is mine, but the power is His.

~PEG RANKIN

TODAY'S OPPORTUNITIES *to* ENCOURAGE

*But encourage each other every day while it is "today." Help each other
so none of you will become hardened because sin has tricked you.*

HEBREWS 3:13 NCV

ach day provides countless opportunities to encourage others and to praise their good works. When we do, we not only spread seeds of joy and happiness, we also follow the commandments of God's Holy Word.

How can we build others up? By celebrating their victories and their accomplishments. So look for the good in others and celebrate the good that you find. When you do, you'll be a powerful force of encouragement in the world . . . and a worthy servant to your God.

*If someone listens or stretches out a hand or whispers a word
of encouragement or attempts to understand a lonely person,
extraordinary things begin to happen.*

~LORETTA GIRZARTIS

*Those who keep speaking about the sun while walking under
a cloudy sky are messengers of hope, the true saints of our day.*

~HENRI J. NOUWEN

ASK *and* RECEIVE

*"Ask, and it will be given to you; seek, and you will find; knock,
and it will be opened to you. For everyone who asks receives, and he
who seeks finds, and to him who knocks it will be opened."*

MATTHEW 7:7–8

*J*esus made it clear to His disciples: they should petition God to meet their needs. So should we. Genuine, heartfelt prayer produces powerful changes in us and in our world. When we lift our hearts to God, we open ourselves to a never-ending source of divine wisdom and infinite love.

Do you have questions about your future that you simply can't answer? Do you have needs that you simply can't meet by yourself? Do you sincerely seek to know God's purpose for your life? If so, ask Him for direction, protection, and strength—and then keep asking Him every day that you live. Whatever your need, no matter how great or small, pray about it and never lose hope. God is not just near; He is here, and He's perfectly capable of answering your prayers. Now it's up to you to ask.

God makes prayer as easy as possible for us. He's completely approachable and available, and He'll never mock or upbraid us for bringing our needs before Him.

~SHIRLEY DOBSON

Forgiveness *at* Home

Let all bitterness, wrath, anger, clamor, and evil speaking be put away from you, with all malice. And be kind to one another, tenderhearted, forgiving one another, just as God in Christ forgave you.

EPHESIANS 4:31–32

Sometimes it's easy to become angry with the people we love most, and sometimes it's hard to forgive them. After all, we know that our family will still love us no matter how angry we become. But while it's easy to become angry at home, it's usually wrong.

The next time you're tempted to lose your temper or to remain angry at a close family member, ask God to help you find the wisdom to forgive. And while you're at it, do your best to calm down sooner rather than later because peace is always beautiful, especially when it's peace in your house.

When something robs you of your peace of mind, ask yourself if it is worth the energy you are expending on it. If not, then put it out of your mind in an act of discipline. Every time the thought of "it" returns, refuse it.

~KAY ARTHUR

The fire of anger, if not quenched by loving forgiveness, will spread and defile and destroy the work of God.

~WARREN WIERSBE

BEYOND ANXIETY

In the multitude of my anxieties within me,
Your comforts delight my soul.

PSALM 94:19

Sometimes trusting God is difficult, especially when we become caught up in the incessant demands of an anxious world. God calls us to live above and beyond anxiety. God calls us to live by faith, not by fear. He instructs us to trust Him completely, this day and forever.

When you feel anxious—and you will—return your thoughts to God's love. Then take your concerns to Him in prayer, and to the best of your ability, leave them there. Whatever "it" is, God is big enough to handle it. Let Him. Now.

> *The moment anxious thoughts invade your mind, go to the Lord in prayer. Look first to God. Then, you will see the cause of your anxiety in a whole new light.*
>
> ~KAY ARTHUR

> *Worry and anxiety are sand in the machinery of life; faith is the oil.*
>
> ~E. STANLEY JONES

> *Anxiety is the natural result when our hopes are centered on anything short of God and His will for us.*
>
> ~BILLY GRAHAM

An Attitude *of* Gratitude

And let the peace of God rule in your hearts, to which
also you were called in one body; and be thankful.

COLOSSIANS 3:15

The beat goes on . . . and on . . . and on . . . Yes, life is both busy and complicated. We have countless responsibilities, some of which begin before sunrise and many of which end long after sunset. Amid the rush and crush of the daily grind, it is easy to lose sight of God and His blessings. But when we forget to slow down and say, "Thank You" to our Maker, we rob ourselves of His presence, His peace, and His joy.

Our task, as believing Christians, is to praise God many times each day. Then, with gratitude in our hearts, we can face our daily duties with the perspective and power that only He can provide.

It is only with gratitude that life becomes rich.
~DIETRICH BONHOEFFER

A sense of gratitude for God's presence in our lives will help
open our eyes to what he has done in the past and what he will
do in the future.

~EMILIE BARNES

His Comforting Hand

Nevertheless God, who comforts the downcast, comforted us.

2 CORINTHIANS 7:6

*J*esus has won the victory, so all Christians should live courageously, including you. If you have been touched by the transforming hand of God's Son, then you have every reason to be confident about your future here on earth and your future in heaven. But even if you are a faithful believer, you may find yourself discouraged by the inevitable disappointments and tragedies that are the price of life here on earth.

If your courage is being tested today, lean upon God's promises. Trust His Son. Remember that God is always near and that He is your protector and your deliverer. When you are worried, anxious, or afraid, call upon Him and accept the touch of His comforting hand. Remember that God rules both mountaintops and valleys—with limitless wisdom and love—now and forever.

> *When I am criticized, injured, or afraid, there is a Father who is ready to comfort me.*
>
> ~MAX LUCADO

> *Put your hand into the hand of God. He gives the calmness and serenity of heart and soul.*
>
> ~MRS. CHARLES E. COWMAN

The BREAD *of* LIFE

Then Jesus said, "I am the bread that gives life. Whoever comes to me will never be hungry, and whoever believes in me will never be thirsty."
JOHN 6:35 NCV

*J*esus Christ, the Son of God, was born into humble circumstances. He walked this earth, not as a ruler of men, but as the Savior of mankind. He was the Son of God, but He wore a crown of thorns. He was the Savior of mankind, yet He was put to death on a rough-hewn cross made of wood. He offered His healing touch to an unsaved world, and yet the same hands that had healed the sick and raised the dead were pierced with nails.

His crucifixion, a torturous punishment that was intended to end His life and His reign, instead became the pivotal event in the history of all humanity.

Jesus is the bread of life. Accept His grace. Share His love. And follow in His footsteps.

> *Our Lord is the Bread of Life. His proportions are perfect. There never was too much or too little of anything about Him. Feed on Him for a well-balanced ration. All the vitamins and calories are there.*
>
> ~VANCE HAVNER

> *Jesus was the perfect reflection of God's nature in every situation He encountered during His time here on earth.*
>
> ~BILL HYBELS

Love Is *a* Choice

Beloved, if God so loved us, we also ought to love one another.

1 John 4:11

The decision to love another person for a lifetime is much more than the simple process of "falling in" or "being swept up." Sometimes we may "fall in love," but it takes work to stay there. Sometimes we may be "swept off our feet," but the "sweeping" is only temporary; sooner or later, if love is to endure, one must plant one's feet firmly on the ground.

Love requires "reaching out," "holding firm," and "lifting up." Love then becomes a decision to honor and care for the other person, come what may. Love, simply put, is a choice.

> *How do you spell love? When you reach the point where the happiness, security, and development of another person is as much of a driving force to you as your own happiness, security, and development, then you have a mature love. True love is spelled G-I-V-E.*
>
> ~Josh McDowell

> *A soul cannot live without loving. It must have something to love, for it was created to love.*
>
> ~Catherine of Siena

The POWER of PRAYER

_~~&..&~_

When a believing person prays, great things happen.
JAMES 5:16 NCV

Prayer is powerful tool for communicating with our Creator; it is an opportunity to commune with the Giver of all things good. Prayer helps us find strength for today and hope for the future. Prayer is not a thing to be taken lightly or to be used infrequently.

The quality of your spiritual life will be in direct proportion to the quality of your prayer life. Prayer changes things, and it changes you. Today, instead of turning things over in your mind, turn them over to God in prayer. Instead of worrying about your next decision, ask God to lead the way. Pray constantly about things great and small. God is listening, and He wants to hear from you now.

> *Where there is much prayer there will be much of the Spirit, and where there is much of the Spirit there will be ever-increasing power.*
>
> ~ANDREW MURRAY

> *The greatest power that God has given to any individual is the power of prayer.*
>
> ~KATHRYN KUHLMAN

Making Time *for* Silence

Be still, and know that I am God.

Psalm 46:10

*S*ilence may indeed be golden, but it is hard for most of us to remain silent for long. God teaches us that it takes stillness to know Him. But stillness is hard.

Do you take time each day for an extended period of silence? And during those precious moments, do you sincerely open your heart to your Creator? If so, you are wise and you are blessed.

This world can be a noisy place, a place filled to the brim with distractions, interruptions, and frustrations. And if you're not careful, the struggles and stresses of everyday living can rob you of the peace that should rightfully be yours because of your personal relationship with Christ. So take time each day to quietly commune with your Savior. When you do, those moments of silence will enable you to participate more fully in the only source of peace that endures: God's peace.

Most of man's trouble comes from his inability to be still.
~Blaise Pascal

The world is full of noise. Might we not set ourselves to learn silence, stillness, solitude?
~Elisabeth Elliot

WORSHIP HIM

---∾⋅⋅⋐---

"God is spirit, and those who worship him must worship in spirit and truth."

What will you choose to worship today? Will you worship your Creator or your possessions? Will you worship your Savior, Jesus Christ, or will you bow down before the false gods of pride and avarice? Will you seek the approval of your God or the approval of your neighbors?

All of mankind is engaged in the practice of worship. Some people choose to worship God and, as a result, reap the joy that He intends for His children. Others distance themselves from God by worshiping such things as earthly possessions or personal gratification. And when they do, they suffer.

Every day provides opportunities to put God where He belongs: at the center of your life. Worship Him— and only Him—today, tomorrow, and always.

Worship is a way of living, a way of seeing the world in the light of God. To worship is to rise to a higher level of existence, to see the world from the point of view of God.

~ABRAHAM JOSHUA HESCHEL

God asks that we worship Him with our concentrated minds as well as with our wills and emotions. A divided and scattered mind is not effective.

~CATHERINE MARSHALL

A HELPING HAND

"Then a Samaritan traveling down the road came to where the hurt man was. When he saw the man, he felt very sorry for him. The Samaritan went to him, poured olive oil and wine on his wounds, and bandaged them. Then he put the hurt man on his own donkey and took him to an inn where he cared for him."

LUKE 10:33–34 NCV

Sometimes we would like to help make the world a better place, but we're not sure how to do it. Jesus told the story of the good Samaritan, a man who helped a fellow traveler when no one else would. We too should be good Samaritans when we find people who need our help.

What can you do to make God's world a better place? You can start by making your own corner of the world a little nicer place to live by sharing kind words and doing good deeds. And then you can take your concerns to God in prayer. Whether you've offered a helping hand or a heartfelt prayer, you've done a lot.

Do all the good you can. By all the means you can. In all the ways you can. In all the places you can. At all the times you can. To all the people you can. As long as ever you can.

~JOHN WESLEY

The WISDOM *to* FORGIVE

*Bear with each other, and forgive each other. If someone does wrong
to you, forgive that person because the Lord forgave you.*

COLOSSIANS 3:13 NCV

Whenever people hurt us—whether emotionally, physically, financially, or otherwise—it's hard to forgive. But God's Word is clear: we must forgive other people, even when we'd rather not. So if you're angry with anybody (or if you're upset by something you yourself have done), it's time to forgive.

God instructs you to treat other people exactly as you wish to be treated. And since you want to be forgiven for the mistakes you make, you must be willing to extend forgiveness to other people for the mistakes they have made.

If you can't seem to forgive someone, you should keep asking God for help you until you do. And of this you can be sure: if you keep asking for God's help, He will give it.

*Have you thought that your willingness to forgive is really your
affirmation of the power of God to do you good?*
~PAULA RINEHART

Having forgiven, I am liberated.
~FATHER LAWRENCE JENCO

A GROWING RELATIONSHIP
with GOD

*But grow in the grace and knowledge of our Lord and Savior Jesus
Christ. To Him be the glory both now and forever.*

2 PETER 3:18

Are you continuing to grow in your love and knowledge of the Lord, or are you "satisfied" with the current state of your spiritual health? Your relationship with God is ongoing; it unfolds day by day, and it offers countless opportunities to grow closer to Him . . . or not.

As each new day unfolds, you are confronted with a wide range of decisions: how you will behave, where you will direct your thoughts, with whom you will associate, and what you will choose to worship. These choices, along with many others like them, are yours and yours alone. How you choose determines how your relationship with God will unfold.

Hopefully you're determined to make yourself a growing Christian. Your Savior deserves no less, and neither, by the way, do you.

> *When it comes to walking with God, there is no such thing as
> instant maturity. God doesn't mass produce His saints. He hand
> tools each one, and it always takes longer than we expected.*
>
> ~CHARLES SWINDOLL

GIVING YOUR WORRIES *to* GOD

_Be humble under God's powerful hand so he will lift you
up when the right time comes. Give all your worries to
him, because he cares about you._

1 PETER 5:6–7 NCV

Perhaps you are uncertain about your future, or perhaps you are simply a worrier by nature. If so, it's time to focus less on your troubles and more on God's promises. And that's as it should be because God is trustworthy and you are protected.

If you are a person with lots of obligations and plenty of responsibilities, it is simply a fact of life: you worry. From time to time, you worry about health, about finances, about safety, about family, and about countless other concerns, some great and some small.

Where is the best place to take your worries? Take them to God. Take your troubles to Him; take your fears to Him; take your doubts to Him; take your weaknesses to Him; take your sorrows to Him . . . and leave them all there. Seek protection from the One who offers you eternal salvation; build your spiritual house upon the rock that cannot be moved.

Don't take tomorrow to bed with you.

~NORMAN VINCENT PEALE

CARING *for the* DOWNTRODDEN

*"I tell you the truth, anything you did for even the least
of my people here, you also did for me."*

MATTHEW 25:40 NCV

How fortunate we are to live in a land of opportunities and possibilities. But for many people around the world, opportunities are scarce, at best. In too many corners of the globe, hardworking men and women struggle mightily to provide food and shelter for their families.

When we care for the downtrodden, we follow in the footsteps of Christ. And when we show compassion for those who suffer, we abide by the commandments of the One who created us. May we, who have been given so much, hear the Word of God and follow it.

*If you want to be truly happy, you won't find it on an endless
quest for more stuff. You'll find it in receiving God's generosity
and the passing that generosity along.*

~BILL HYBELS

*A cup that is already full cannot have more added to it. In
order to receive the further good to which we are entitled, we
must give of that which we have.*

~MARGARET BECKER

Moving On

"You have heard that it was said, 'Love your neighbor and hate your enemies.' But I say to you, love your enemies. Pray for those who hurt you."

MATTHEW 5:43–44 NCV

In Luke 6:37, Jesus instructs, "Judge not, and you shall not be judged. Condemn not, and you shall not be condemned. Forgive, and you will be forgiven." Sometimes people can be discourteous and cruel. Sometimes people can be unfair, unkind, and unappreciative. Sometimes people become angry and frustrated. So what's a Christian to do? God's answer is straightforward: forgive, forget, and move on.

Today and every day, make sure that you're quick to forgive others for their shortcomings. And when other people misbehave (as they most certainly will from time to time), don't pay too much attention. Just forgive those people as quickly as you can, and try to move on as quickly as you can.

A keen sense of humor helps us to overlook the unbecoming, understand the unconventional, tolerate the unpleasant, overcome the unexpected, and outlast the unbearable.

~BILLY GRAHAM

The Son of Encouragement

Good people's words will help many others.

PROVERBS 10:21 NCV

*B*arnabas, a man whose name meant "son of encouragement," was a leader in the early Christian church. He was known for his kindness and for his ability to encourage others. Because of Barnabas, many people were introduced to Christ. And today, as believers living in a difficult world, we must seek to imitate the "son of encouragement."

We imitate Barnabas when we speak kind words to our families and our friends. We imitate Barnabas when our actions give credence to our beliefs. We imitate Barnabas when we are generous with our possessions and our praise. We imitate Barnabas when we give hope to the hopeless and encouragement to the downtrodden.

Today, be like Barnabas: become a source of encouragement to those who cross your path. When you do, you will quite literally change the world, one person—and one moment—at a time.

God is still in the process of dispensing gifts, and He uses ordinary individuals like us to develop those gifts in other people.
~HOWARD HENDRICKS

FRIENDSHIPS THAT HONOR GOD

Blessed is the man who walks not in the counsel of the ungodly, nor stands in the path of sinners, nor sits in the seat of the scornful.

PSALM 1:1

ecause we tend to become like our friends, we must choose our friends carefully. Because our friends influence us in ways that are both subtle and powerful, we must ensure that our friendships are pleasing to God. Some friendships help us honor God; these friendships should be nurtured. Other friendships place us in situations where we are tempted to dishonor God by disobeying His commandments; friendships such as these have the potential to do us great harm.

When we spend our days in the presence of godly believers, we are blessed, not only by those friends, but also by our Creator.

> *Friends are like a quilt with lots of different shapes, sizes, colors, and patterns of fabric. But the end result brings you warmth and comfort in a support system that makes your life richer and fuller.*
>
> ~SUZANNE DALE EZELL

> *I have found that the closer I am to the godly people around me, the easier it is for me to live a righteous life because they hold me accountable.*
>
> ~JOHN MACARTHUR

Hope *for the* Journey

*So we may boldly say: "The Lord is my helper; I
will not fear. What can man do to me?"*

HEBREWS 13:6

Circumstances should never dictate our attitudes toward life. Because we are saved by a risen Christ, we can have hope for the future, no matter how desperate our circumstances may seem. After all, God has promised that we are His throughout eternity. And He has told us that we must place our hopes in Him.

Today, summon the courage to follow God. Even if the path seems difficult, even if your heart is fearful, trust your heavenly Father and follow Him. Trust Him with your day and your life. Do His work, care for His children, and share His good news. Let Him guide your steps. He will not lead you astray.

> *God knows that the strength that comes from wrestling with
> our fear will give us wings to fly.*
>
> ~PAULA RINEHART

> *Why rely on yourself and fall? Cast yourself upon His arm. Be
> not afraid. He will not let you slip. Cast yourself in confidence.
> He will receive you and heal you.*
>
> ~ST. AUGUSTINE

The ULTIMATE PROTECTION

The LORD himself will go before you. He will be with you; he will not leave you or forget you. Don't be afraid and don't worry.

DEUTERONOMY 31:8 NCV

God has promised to protect us, and He intends to fulfill His promise. In a world filled with dangers and temptations, God is the ultimate armor. In a world filled with misleading messages, God's Word is the ultimate truth. In a world filled with more frustrations than we can count, God's Son offers the ultimate peace.

Will you accept God's peace and wear God's armor against the dangers of our world? Hopefully so, because when you do, you can live courageously, knowing that you possess the ultimate protection: God's unfailing love for you.

Our future may look fearfully intimidating, yet we can look up to the Engineer of the Universe, confident that nothing escapes His attention or slips out of the control of those strong hands.

~ELISABETH ELLIOT

Kept by the power of God—that is the only safety.

~OSWALD CHAMBERS

Commissioned *to* Share *the* Good News

*"Go therefore and make disciples of all the nations, baptizing them
in the name of the Father and of the Son and of the Holy Spirit,
teaching them to observe all things that I have commanded you;
and lo, I am with you always, even to the end of the age." Amen.*

MATTHEW 28:19–20

After His resurrection, Jesus addressed His disciples. As recorded in Matthew 28, Christ instructed His followers to share His message with the world. This Great Commission applies to Christians of every generation, including our own.

As believers, we are called to share the good news of Jesus with our families, our neighbors, and the world. Christ commanded His disciples to become fishers of men. We must do likewise, and we must do so today. Tomorrow may be too late.

*Our commission is quite specific. We are told to be His witness
to all nations. For us, as His disciples, to refuse any part of this
commission frustrates the love of Jesus Christ, the Son of God.*

~CATHERINE MARSHALL

LET *the* CELEBRATION BEGIN

"These things I have spoken to you, that My joy may remain in you, and that your joy may be full."

JOHN 15:11

St. Augustine wrote, "The Christian ought to be alleluia from head to foot." Sometimes, however, even the most dedicated Christians can occasionally forget to celebrate each day for what it is—a priceless gift from God.

Today, let us be filled with joy, putting smiles on our faces and kind words on our lips. After all, this is God's day, and He has given us clear instructions for its use. He commands us to rejoice and be glad. So, without further ado, let the celebration begin!

Joy can be the echo of God's life within you.

~DUANE PEDERSON

It is the definition of joy to be able to offer back to God the essence of what he's placed in you, be that creativity or a love of ideas or a compassionate heart or the gift of hospitality.

~PAULA RINEHART

Joy is the simplest form of gratitude.

~KARL BARTH

FALLING *in* LOVE . . . *with* GOD

You shall love the LORD your God with all your heart,
with all your soul, and with all your strength.

DEUTERONOMY 6:5

Vance Havner observed, "The church has no greater need than to fall in love with Jesus all over again." How true. When churches (and their members!) fall in love with God and His only begotten Son, great things happen.

When we worship God faithfully and obediently, we invite His love into our hearts. When we truly love God, we allow Him to rule over our days and our lives. In turn, we grow to love God even more deeply as we sense His love for us.

Today, open your heart to the Father and to the Son. And let your obedience be a fitting response to their never-ending love.

> *When we develop an authentic love relationship with God, we will not be able to keep Him compartmentalized in "churchy," religious categories.*
>
> ~BETH MOORE

> *When our heart's desire is to please our Lord because we love Him, there will be no time for second thoughts or second opinions.*
>
> ~WARREN WIERSBE

The SOURCE *of* ALL COMFORT

I was very worried, but you comforted me.

PSALM 94:19 NCV

We are wise to remember the words of Jesus, who, when He walked on the waters, reassured His disciples, saying, "Take courage! It is I. Don't be afraid" (Matthew 14:27 NIV). Then, with Christ on His throne—and with trusted friends and loving family members at our sides—we can face our fears with courage and with faith.

Are you facing a difficult challenge? If so, remember the ultimate Source of your comfort, and start talking to Him right now.

When I am criticized, injured, or afraid, there is a Father who is ready to comfort me.

~MAX LUCADO

No journey is complete that does not lead through some dark valleys. We can properly comfort others only with the comfort we ourselves have been given by God.

~VANCE HAVNER

He is always thinking about us. We are before his eyes. The Lord's eye never sleeps, but is always watching out for our welfare. We are continually on his heart.

~C. H. SPURGEON

HE RENEWS OUR STRENGTH

*Anxiety in the heart of man causes depression,
but a good word makes it glad.*

PROVERBS 12:25

When we fail to meet the expectations of others (or, for that matter, the expectations that we have set for ourselves), we may be tempted to abandon hope. Thankfully, on those cloudy days when our strength is sapped and our faith is shaken, there exists a source from which we can draw courage and wisdom. That source is God.

When we seek to form a more intimate and dynamic relationship with our Creator, He renews our spirits and restores our souls. God's promise is made clear in Ezekiel 36:26, "I will give you a new heart and put a new spirit within you." And upon this promise we can—and should—depend.

Don't let aridity distress you: perfection has nothing to do with such things—only with virtues. Your devotion will come back when you are least expecting it.

~ST. TERESA OF AVILA

The same God who empowered Samson, Gideon, and Paul seeks to empower my life and your life, because God hasn't changed.

~BILL HYBELS

Strength *for* Any Challenge

"I have carried you since you were born; I have taken care of you from your birth. Even when you are old, I will be the same. Even when your hair has turned gray, I will take care of you. I made you and will take care of you. I will carry you and save you."

ISAIAH 46:3–4 NCV

God's love and support never change. From the cradle to the grave, God has promised to give you the strength to meet any challenge. God has promised to lift you up and guide your steps if you let Him. God has promised that when you entrust your life to Him completely and without reservation, He will give you the courage to face any trial and the wisdom to live in His righteousness.

God's hand uplifts those who turn their hearts and prayers to Him. Will you count yourself among that number? Will you accept God's peace and wear God's armor against the temptations and distractions of our dangerous world? If you do, you can live courageously and optimistically, knowing that you have been forever touched by the loving, unfailing, uplifting hand of God.

He can accomplish anything He chooses to do. If He ever asks you to do something, He Himself will enable you to do it.
~HENRY BLACKABY

OUR ROCK *in* TURBULENT TIMES

*And he said: "The LORD is my rock and my fortress and my
deliverer; the God of my strength, in whom I will trust."*
2 SAMUEL 22:2–3

As believers, we know that God loves us and
that He will protect us. In times of hardship,
God offers to comfort us; in times of sorrow, He offers
to dry our tears. The words of Jesus offer us comfort:
"These things I have spoken to you, that in Me you may
have peace. In the world you will have tribulation; but
be of good cheer, I have overcome the world" (John
16:33).

When we are troubled, or weak, or sorrowful, God
is always with us. We must build our lives on the rock
that cannot be shaken; we must trust in God. And then
we must get on with the hard work of tackling our
problems, because if we don't, who will?

The Rock of Ages is the great sheltering encirclement.
~OSWALD CHAMBERS

*We all go through pain and sorrow, but the presence of God,
like a warm, comforting blanket, can shield us and protect us,
and allow the deep inner joy to surface, even in the most dev-
astating circumstances.*

~BARBARA JOHNSON

WHAT DOESN'T CHANGE

Jesus Christ is the same yesterday, today, and forever.
HEBREWS 13:8 NCV

Some things change and some things do not. Our world is in constant flux. Our God is the same yesterday, today, and tomorrow.

At times, the world seems to be trembling beneath our feet. But we can be comforted in the knowledge that our heavenly Father is the rock that cannot be shaken. His Word promises, "I am the LORD, I do not change" (Malachi 3:6).

Every day that we live, we mortals encounter a multitude of changes—some good, some not so good, some downright disheartening. On those occasions when we must endure life-changing personal losses that leave us breathless, there is a place we can turn for comfort and assurance—we can turn to God. When we do, our loving, heavenly Father stands ready to protect us, comfort us, guide us, and, in time, heal us.

In a world kept chaotic by change, you will eventually discover, as I have, that this is one of the most precious qualities of the God we are looking for: He doesn't change.
~BILL HYBELS

CONFIDENT CHRISTIANITY

You are my hope, O Lord GOD; You are my trust from my youth.

PSALM 71:5

We live in a world that fosters insecurity and doubts. But because we are Christians, we have many reasons to be confident. God loves us, Christ has saved us, and we have far more blessings than we can count. Yet sometimes even the most devout believers can become discouraged. Discouragement, however, is not God's way; He is a God of possibility, not negativity.

Are you a confident Christian? You should be. God's grace is eternal and His promises are unambiguous. So count your blessings, not your hardships. And live courageously. God is the Giver of all things good, and He watches over you today and forever.

> *If our minds are stayed upon God, His peace will rule the affairs entertained by our minds. If, on the other hand, we allow our minds to dwell on the cares of this world, God's peace will be far from our thoughts.*
>
> ~WOODROLL KROLL

> *There is no other method of living piously and justly than that of depending upon God.*
>
> ~JOHN CALVIN

Faith *to* Share

That is why I was chosen to tell the Good News and to be an apostle. (I am telling the truth; I am not lying.) I was chosen to teach those who are not Jews to believe and to know the truth.

1 Timothy 2:7 NCV

If heaven is such a wonderful place (and it is!), why doesn't God simply take us there when we become believers? The answer is simple: we still have work to do. And an important part of that work involves our faith—building it and sharing it.

When a suffering woman sought healing by merely touching the hem of His cloak, Jesus replied, "Daughter, be of good comfort; thy faith hath made thee whole" (Matthew 9:22 KJV). The message to believers of every generation is clear: we must live by faith today and every day.

How can you strengthen your faith? Through praise, worship, Bible study, and prayer. And as your faith becomes stronger, you will find ways to share it with your friends, your family, and the world. And that, by the way, is exactly what God wants you to do.

Our faith grows by expression. If we want to keep our faith, we must share it. We must act.

~Billy Graham

The CORNERSTONE

Let us run with endurance the race that is set before us, looking unto Jesus, the author and finisher of our faith, who for the joy that was set before Him endured the cross, despising the shame, and has sat down at the right hand of the throne of God.

HEBREWS 12:1–2

God has given you the gift of eternal life through His Son. In response to God's priceless gift, you are instructed to focus your thoughts, prayers, and energies upon God and His only begotten Son. Is Christ the focus of your life? Are you fired up with enthusiasm for Him? Are you an energized Christian who allows God's Son to reign over every aspect of your day? Make no mistake: that's exactly what God intends for you to do.

To stay focused on Christ, you must resist the subtle yet powerful temptation to become a "spiritual dabbler." A person who dabbles in the Christian faith is unwilling to place God above all other things. Resist that temptation; make God the cornerstone and the touchstone of your life. When you do, He will give you all the strength and wisdom you need to live victoriously for Him.

Give me the person who says, "This one thing I do, and not these fifty things I dabble in."

~D. L. MOODY

Forgiveness *and* Freedom

> *"And forgive us our sins, for we also forgive
> everyone who is indebted to us."*
>
> Luke 11:4

*A*s a believer who is the recipient of God's forgiveness, how should you behave toward others? Should you forgive them, just as God has forgiven you, or should you remain embittered and resentful?

God's power to forgive, like His love, is infinite. Despite your shortcomings, despite your sins, God offers you immediate forgiveness and eternal life when you accept Christ as your Savior.

God's Word instructs you to forgive others. When you do, you not only obey God's command, you also free yourself from a prison of your own making . . . and that's a very nice thing to do for yourself.

The well of God's forgiveness never runs dry.

~Grady Nutt

Forgiveness is actually the best revenge because it not only sets us free from the person we forgive, but it frees us to move into all that God has in store for us.

~Stormie Omartian

SHARING *the* JOY

*Every day is hard for those who suffer, but a
happy heart is like a continual feast.*

PROVERBS 15:15 NCV

Christ promises us lives of abundance and joy,
but He does not force His joy upon us. We must
claim His joy for ourselves, and when we do, Jesus, in
turn, fills our spirits with His power and His love. Few
things in life are more sad, or, for that matter, more
absurd, than a grumpy Christian.

How can we receive from Christ the joy that is rightfully ours? By giving Him what is rightfully His: our
hearts and our souls.

When we earnestly commit ourselves to the Savior
of mankind, when we place Jesus at the center of our
lives and trust Him as our personal Savior, He will
transform us, not just for today, but for all eternity.
Then we, as God's children, can share Christ's joy and
His message with a world that needs both.

Sour godliness is the devil's religion.

~JOHN WESLEY

*The greatest honor you can give Almighty God is to live gladly
and joyfully because of the knowledge of His love.*

~JULIANA OF NORWICH

The ULTIMATE INSTRUCTION MANUAL

*He who despises the word will be destroyed, but he who
fears the commandment will be rewarded.*

PROVERBS 13:13

God's commandments are not suggestions. They are given by a loving God who wants the best for His children.

The Holy Bible contains thorough instructions that, if followed, lead to fulfillment, righteousness, and salvation. But if we choose to ignore God's commandments, the results are as predictable as they are tragic.

A righteous life has many components: faith, honesty, generosity, love, kindness, humility, gratitude, and worship, to name but a few. If we seek to follow the steps of our Savior, Jesus Christ, we must seek to live according to His commandments. Let us follow God's commandments, and let us conduct our lives in such a way that we might be shining examples for those who have not yet found Christ.

Bible history is filled with people who began the race with great success but failed at the end because they disregarded God's rules.

~WARREN WIERSBE

His Joy . . . *and* Ours

Rejoice in the Lord always. Again I will say, rejoice!
PHILIPPIANS 4:4

Christ made it clear: He intends that His joy should become our joy. Yet sometimes, amid the inevitable hustle and bustle of life, we can forfeit—albeit temporarily—the joy of Christ as we wrestle with the challenges of daily living.

Billy Graham correctly observed, "When Jesus Christ is the source of our joy, no words can describe it." And C. S. Lewis noted, "Joy is the serious business of heaven." So here's a prescription for better spiritual health: open the door of your soul to Christ. When you do, He will give you His peace and His joy, and you'll be eternally grateful that He did.

> *When I think of God, my heart is so full of joy that the notes leap and dance as they leave my pen; and since God has given me a cheerful heart, I serve him with a cheerful spirit.*
> ~FRANZ JOSEPH HAYDN

> *As I contemplate all the sacrifices required in order to live a life that is totally focused on Jesus Christ and His eternal kingdom, the joy seeps out of my heart onto my face in a smile of deep satisfaction.*
> ~ANNE GRAHAM LOTZ

The TREASURE HUNT

Do not love the world or the things in the world. If you love the world, the love of the Father is not in you.

1 JOHN 2:15 NCV

$\mathcal{A}$ ll of mankind is engaged in a colossal, world-wide treasure hunt. Many people seek treasure from earthly sources, treasures such as material wealth or public acclaim. But the smart and successful ones seek God's treasures by making Him the cornerstone of their lives.

What kind of treasure hunter are you? Are you so caught up in the demands of everyday living that you sometimes allow the search for worldly treasures to become your primary focus? If so, it's time to reorganize your daily to-do list by placing God in His rightful place: first. Don't allow anyone or anything to separate you from your heavenly Father and His only begotten Son.

The world's treasures are difficult to find and difficult to keep; God's treasures are ever present and everlasting. Which treasures will you claim as your own?

Nothing is more foolish than a security built upon the world and its promises, for they are all vanity and a lie.

~MATTHEW HENRY

Why is love of gold more potent than love of souls?

~LOTTIE MOON

TOTAL TRUST

Trust in Him at all times, you people; pour out your heart before Him; God is a refuge for us.

PSALM 62:8

On the sunnier days of life, we find it easy to praise God, trust Him, and give thanks. But when we endure the storms of bitterness and despair, trusting God is more difficult.

The next time you find your courage tested to the limit, lean upon God's promises. Trust His Son. When you are worried, anxious, or afraid, call upon Him. God can manage your troubles infinitely better than you can, so turn them over to Him. Remember that God rules both the sunny days and the darker ones with limitless wisdom and love now and forever.

> *I'm discovering that the first step toward a vital, trusting relationship with God is speaking the truth—bringing myself out of the shadows and talking honestly to my Father.*
>
> ~SHEILA WALSH

> *Trusting God completely means having faith that he knows what is best for your life. You expect him to keep his promises, help you with problems, and do the impossible when necessary.*
>
> ~RICK WARREN

WHEN ANGER IS OKAY

The face of the LORD is against those who do evil.

PSALM 34:16

Sometimes anger can be a good thing. In Matthew 21, we are told how Christ responded when He confronted the evildoings of those who had invaded His Father's house of worship:

"Then Jesus went into the temple of God and drove out all those who bought and sold in the temple, and overturned the tables of the money changers and the seats of those who sold doves. And He said to them, 'It is written, "My house shall be called a house of prayer," but you have made it a "den of thieves"'" (vv. 12–13). Thus, Jesus demonstrated that righteous indignation is an appropriate response to evil.

When you come face-to-face with the devil's handiwork, don't be satisfied to remain safely on the sidelines. Instead, follow in the footsteps of your Savior. Jesus never compromised with evil, and neither should you.

There is a holy anger, excited by zeal, that moves us to reprove with warmth those whom our mildness failed to correct.
~JEAN BAPTISTE DE LA SALLE

We cannot love God if we do not hate evil.

~ST. JEROME

The Promise of Power

When we were baptized, we were buried with Christ and shared his death. So, just as Christ was raised from the dead by the wonderful power of the Father, we also can live a new life.

ROMANS 6:4 NCV

When you invite Christ to rule over your heart, you avail yourself of His power. And make no mistake: you and Christ, working together, can do miraculous things. In fact, miraculous things are exactly what Christ intends for you to do, but He won't force you to do great things on His behalf. The decision to become a full-fledged participant in His power is a decision that you must make for yourself.

The words of John 14:12 make this promise: when you put absolute faith in Christ, you can share in His power. Today, trust the Savior's promise and expect a miracle in His name.

> *The Christian life is not simply following principles but being empowered to fulfill our purpose: knowing and exalting Christ.*
>
> ~FRANKLIN GRAHAM

> *The amount of power you experience to live a victorious, triumphant Christian life is directly proportional to the freedom you give the Spirit to be Lord of your life!*
>
> ~ANNE GRAHAM LOTZ

The Promise of Contentment

*I am not telling you this because I need anything. I have
learned to be satisfied with the things I have and with
everything that happens. I know how to live when I am poor,
and I know how to live when I have plenty. I have learned the
secret of being happy at any time in everything that happens.*

PHILIPPIANS 4:11–12 NCV

If we don't find contentment in God, we will never find it anywhere else. But if we seek Him and obey Him, we will be blessed with an inner peace that is beyond human understanding. Genuine contentment is a gift from God to those who trust Him and follow His commandments.

Our modern world seems preoccupied with the search for happiness. We are bombarded with messages telling us that happiness depends upon the acquisition of material possessions. These messages are false. Enduring peace is not the result of our acquisitions; it is a spiritual gift from God to those who obey Him and accept His will.

When God dwells at the center of our lives, peace and contentment will belong to us just as surely as we belong to God.

*True contentment comes from godliness in the heart, not from
wealth in the hand.*

~WARREN WIERSBE

CELEBRATING OTHERS

So encourage each other and give each other strength, just as you are doing now.

1 THESSALONIANS 5:11 NCV

*D*o you delight in the victories of others? You should. Each day provides countless opportunities to encourage others and praise their good works. When you do, you not only spread seeds of joy and happiness, you also obey the commandments of God's Holy Word.

As Christians, we are called upon to spread the good news of Christ, and we are also called to spread a message of encouragement and hope to the world. Today, let us be cheerful Christians with smiles on our faces and encouraging words on our lips. By blessing others, we also bless ourselves, and, at the same time, we do honor to the One who gave His life for us.

My special friends, who know me so well and love me anyway, give me daily encouragement to keep on.

~EMILIE BARNES

A lot of people have gone further than they thought they could because someone else thought they could.

~ZIG ZIGLAR

Peace *to* You

Peace, peace to you, and peace to your helpers!
For your God helps you.

1 Chronicles 12:18

Sometimes our struggles are simply manifestations of the inner conflict we feel when we stray from God's path.

Have you found the genuine peace that can be yours through Christ? Or are you still rushing after the illusion of "peace and happiness" that the world promises but cannot deliver? Today, as a gift to yourself and to your loved ones, claim the inner peace that is your spiritual birthright: the peace of Jesus Christ.

Earthly peace can, and should, be yours. But the spiritual peace that stems from your personal relationship with Jesus must be yours if you are to receive the eternal abundance of our Lord. Claim that abundance today.

If the Living Logos of God has the power to create and sustain the universe, He is more than able to sustain your marriage and your ministry, your faith and your finances, your hope and your health.

~Anne Graham Lotz

The CHOICE *to* FORGIVE

"You have heard that it was said, 'You shall love your neighbor and hate your enemy.' But I say to you, love your enemies, bless those who curse you, do good to those who hate you, and pray for those who spitefully use you and persecute you, that you may be sons of your Father in heaven."

MATTHEW 5:43–45

ife is filled with choices, and one of the most important choices we can ever make is the choice to forgive. And make no mistake: forgiveness is a choice. We can either choose to forgive those who have injured us, or not. When we obey God by offering forgiveness to His children, we are blessed. But when we allow bitterness and resentment to poison our hearts, we are tortured by our own shortsightedness.

Do you harbor resentment against anyone? If so, you are faced with an important decision: whether to forgive the person who has hurt you. God's instructions are clear: He commands you to forgive. And the time to forgive is now because tomorrow may be too late . . . for you.

Jesus is the only One Who makes not only our sins but also the sins of others against us forgivable.

~ANNE GRAHAM LOTZ

FREELY GIVE

—⊰⋅⊱—

So let each one give as he purposes in his heart, not grudgingly
or of necessity; for God loves a cheerful giver.

2 CORINTHIANS 9:7

The words are familiar to those who study God's Word: "Freely you have received, freely give." As followers of Christ, we have been given so much by God. In return, we must give freely of our time, our possessions, our testimonies, and our love.

Your salvation was earned at a terrible price: Christ gave His life for you on the cross at Calvary. Christ's gift is priceless, yet when you accept Jesus as your personal Savior, His gift of eternal life costs you nothing. From those to whom much has been given, much is required. And because you have received the gift of salvation, you are now called by God to be a cheerful, generous steward of the gifts He has placed under your care.

Today and every day, let Christ's words be your guide and let His eternal love fill your heart. When you do, your stewardship will be a reflection of your love for Him, and that's exactly as it should be. After all, He loved you first.

As faithful stewards of what we have, ought we not to give earnest thought to our staggering surplus?

~ELISABETH ELLIOT

ENTRUSTING OUR LIVES *to* HIM

*"Father, if it is Your will, take this cup away from Me;
nevertheless not My will, but Yours, be done."*

LUKE 22:42

*A*s human beings with limited understanding, we can never fully comprehend the will of God. But as believers in a benevolent God, we must always trust the will of our heavenly Father.

Before His crucifixion, Jesus went to the Mount of Olives and opened His heart to the Father. Jesus knew of the torture that He must soon endure, but He also knew that God's will must be done.

We, like our Savior, face trials that bring fear and trembling to the very depths of our souls, but like Christ, we must ultimately seek God's will, not our own. When we entrust our lives to Him completely and without reservation, He gives us the strength to meet any challenge, the courage to face any trial, and the wisdom to live in His righteousness.

The will of God is the most delicious and delightful thing in the universe.

~HANNAH WHITALL SMITH

To know the will of God is the greatest knowledge! To do the will of God is the greatest achievement.

~GEORGE W. TRUETT

HOPE *for* TODAY

You have this faith and love because of your hope, and what you hope for is kept safe for you in heaven. You learned about this hope when you heard the message about the truth, the Good News.

COLOSSIANS 1:5 NCV

Despite God's promises, despite Christ's love, and despite our countless blessings, we frail human beings can still lose hope from time to time. When we do, we need the encouragement of Christian friends, the life-changing power of prayer, and the healing truth of God's Holy Word. If we find ourselves falling into the spiritual traps of worry and discouragement, we should seek the healing touch of Jesus and the encouraging words of fellow Christians.

Even though this world can be a place of trials and struggles, God has promised us peace, joy, and eternal life if we give ourselves to Him. And God keeps His promises today, tomorrow, and forever.

> *The most profane word we use is "hopeless." When you say a situation or person is hopeless, you are slamming the door in the face of God.*
>
> ~KATHY TROCCOLI

> *What oxygen is to the lungs, such is hope to the meaning of life.*
>
> ~EMIL BRUNNER

The POWER *of* PERSEVERANCE

There is one thing I always do. Forgetting the past and straining toward what is ahead, I keep trying to reach the goal and get the prize for which God called me.

PHILIPPIANS 3:13–14 NCV

A well-lived life calls for preparation, determination, and lots of perseverance. As an example of perfect perseverance, we Christians need look no further than our Savior, Jesus Christ. Jesus finished what He began. Despite His suffering, despite the shame of the cross, Jesus was steadfast in His faithfulness to God. We too must remain faithful, especially during times of hardship. Sometimes God may answer our prayers with silence, and when He does, we must patiently persevere.

Are you facing a tough situation? If so, remember this: whatever your problem, God can handle it. Your job is to keep persevering until He does.

If things are tough, remember that every flower that ever bloomed had to go through a whole lot of dirt to get there.

~BARBARA JOHNSON

Only the man who follows the command of Jesus single-mindedly and unresistingly lets his yoke rest upon him, finds his burden easy, and under its gentle pressure receives the power to persevere in the right way.

~DIETRICH BONHOEFFER

JUST PASSING THROUGH

For whatever is born of God overcomes the world. And this is the victory that has overcome the world—our faith.

1 JOHN 5:4

Sometimes the troubles of this old world are easier to tolerate when we remind ourselves that heaven is our true home. An old hymn contains the words, "This world is not my home; I'm just passing through." Thank goodness!

This crazy world can be a place of trouble and danger. Thankfully, God has offered you a permanent home in heaven, a place of unimaginable glory, a place that your heavenly Father has already prepared for you.

In John 16:33, Jesus tells us He has overcome the troubles of this world. We should trust Him, and we should obey His commandments. When we do, we can withstand any problem, knowing that our troubles are temporary, but that heaven is not.

All those who look to draw their satisfaction from the wells of the world—pleasure, popularity, position, possessions, politics, power, prestige, finances, family, friends, fame, fortune, career, children, church, clubs, sports, sex, success, recognition, reputation, religion, education, entertainment, exercise, honors, health, hobbies—will soon be thirsty again!

~ANNE GRAHAM LOTZ

Trusting God's Leading

My brethren, count it all joy when you fall into various trials, knowing that the testing of your faith produces patience. But let patience have its perfect work, that you may be perfect and complete, lacking nothing.

James 1:2–4

Whether we realize it or not, times of adversity can be times of intense personal and spiritual growth. Our difficult days are also times when we can learn and relearn some of life's most important lessons.

The next time you experience a difficult moment, a difficult day, or a difficult year, ask yourself this question: "Where is God leading me?" In times of struggle and sorrow, you can be certain that God is leading you to a place of His choosing. Your duty is to watch, pray, listen, and follow.

When I feel like circumstances are spiraling downward in my life, God taught me that whether I'm right side up or upside down, I need to turn those circumstances over to Him. He is the only one who can bring balance into my life.

~Carole Lewis

Many men owe the grandeur of their lives to their tremendous difficulties.

~C. H. Spurgeon

Hope During Times *of* Change

"Therefore do not worry about tomorrow, for tomorrow will worry about its own things. Sufficient for the day is its own trouble."

MATTHEW 6:34

There is no doubt that your world is constantly changing. So today's question is this: How will you manage all those changes? Will you do your best and trust God with the rest, or will you spend fruitless hours worrying about things you can't control, while doing precious little else? The answer to these simple questions will help determine the direction and quality of your life.

The best way to confront change is head-on and with God by your side. The same God who created the universe will protect you if you ask Him, so ask Him—and then serve Him with willing hands and a trusting heart. When you do, you may rest assured that while the world changes moment by moment, God's love endures—unfathomable and unchanging—forever.

When we are young, change is a treat, but as we grow older, change becomes a threat. But when Jesus Christ is in control of your life, you need never fear change or decay.

~WARREN WIERSBE

Sharing Words *of* Hope

*Let us think about each other and help each other
to show love and do good deeds.*

HEBREWS 10:24 NCV

Hope, like other human emotions, is contagious. When we associate with hope-filled
Christians, we are encouraged by their faith and opti-
mism. But if we spend too much time in the company
of naysayers and pessimists, our attitudes, like theirs,
tend to be cynical and negative.

Are you a hopeful, optimistic, encouraging believer?
And do you associate with like-minded people?
Hopefully so. As a faithful follower of the One from
Galilee, you have every reason to be hopeful, and you
have every reason to share your hopes with others. So
today, look for reasons to celebrate God's endless blessings. And while you're at it, look for people who will
join you in the celebration. You'll be better for their
company, and they'll be better for yours.

*The glory of friendship is not the outstretched hand, or the
kindly smile, or the joy of companionship. It is the spiritual
inspiration that comes to one when he discovers that someone else believes in him and is willing to trust him with his
friendship.*

~CORRIE TEN BOOM

GOD'S FORGIVENESS

*If we confess our sins, He is faithful and just to forgive us our sins
and to cleanse us from all unrighteousness.*

1 JOHN 1:9

The Bible promises you this: when you ask God for forgiveness, He will give it. No questions asked; no explanations required.

God's power to forgive, like His love, is infinite. Despite your sins, God offers immediate forgiveness. And it's time to take Him up on His offer.

When it comes to forgiveness, God doesn't play favorites and neither should you. You should forgive all the people who have harmed you, not just the people who have asked for forgiveness or the ones who have made restitution. Complete forgiveness is God's way, and it should be your way too. Anything less is not enough.

The sequence of forgiveness and then repentance, rather than repentance and then forgiveness, is crucial for understanding the gospel of grace.

~BRENNAN MANNING

For God is, indeed, a wonderful Father who longs to pour out His mercy upon us, and whose majesty is so great that He can transform us from deep within.

~TERESA OF AVILA

His Generosity . . . *and* Yours

But God demonstrates His own love toward us, in that
while we were still sinners, Christ died for us.

ROMANS 5:8

Christ showed His generous love for us by willingly sacrificing His own life so that we might have eternal life. We, as Christ's followers, are challenged to share His love. And when we walk each day with Jesus—and obey the commandments found in God's Holy Word—we are worthy ambassadors for Him.

Just as Christ has been and will always be the ultimate friend to His flock, so should we be Christlike in our love and generosity to those in need. When we share the love of Christ, we share a priceless gift. As His servants, we must do no less.

The measure of a life, after all, is not its duration but its donation.

~CORRIE TEN BOOM

The world says, the more you take, the more you have. Christ says, the more you give, the more you are.

~FREDERICK BUECHNER

BLESSED FOREVER

For all have sinned, and fall short of the glory of God, being justified freely by His grace through the redemption that is in Christ Jesus.

ROMANS 3:23–24

Someone has said that GRACE stands for God's Redemption At Christ's Expense. It's true—God sent His Son so that we might be redeemed from our sins. In doing so, our heavenly Father demonstrated His infinite mercy and His infinite love. We have received countless gifts from God, but none can compare with the gift of salvation. God's grace is the ultimate gift, and we owe Him the ultimate in thanksgiving.

The gift of eternal life is the priceless possession of everyone who accepts God's Son as Lord and Savior. We return our Savior's love by welcoming Him into our hearts and sharing His message and His love. When we do, we are blessed today and forever.

> *There is no secret that can separate you from God's love; there is no secret that can separate you from His blessings; there is no secret that is worth keeping from His grace.*
>
> ~SERITA ANN JAKES

> *God doesn't call the qualified, He qualifies the called.*
>
> ~ANONYMOUS

ALWAYS FORGIVING

Then Peter came to Him and said, "Lord, how often shall my brother sin against me, and I forgive him? Up to seven times?" Jesus said to him, "I do not say to you, up to seven times, but up to seventy times seven."

MATTHEW 18:21–22

How often should we forgive other people? More times than we can count (Matthew 18:21–22). That's a tall order, but we must remember that it's an order from God—an order that must be obeyed.

In God's curriculum, forgiveness isn't optional; it's a required course. Sometimes we have a very difficult time forgiving the people who have hurt us, but if we don't find it in our hearts to forgive them, we not only hurt ourselves, we also disobey our Father in heaven. So we must forgive—and keep forgiving—for as long as we live.

God gives us permission to forget our past and the understanding to live our present. He said He will remember our sins no more (Psalm 103:11–12).

~SERITA ANN JAKES

What makes a Christian a Christian is not perfection but forgiveness.

~MAX LUCADO

The GREATEST AMONG US

So prepare your minds for service and have self-control.

1 PETER 1:13 NCV

*J*esus teaches that the most esteemed men and women are not the leaders of society or the captains of industry. To the contrary, Jesus teaches that the greatest among us are those who choose to minister and serve.

Today, you may feel the temptation to build yourself up in the eyes of your neighbors. Resist that temptation. Instead, serve your neighbors quietly and without fanfare. Then, when you have done your best to serve your community and serve your God, you can rest comfortably knowing that in the eyes of God, you have achieved greatness. And God's eyes, after all, are the only ones that really count.

Service is the pathway to real significance.

~RICK WARREN

We can love Jesus in the hungry, the naked, and the destitute who are dying. . . . If you love, you will be willing to serve. And you will find Jesus in the distressing disguise of the poor.

~MOTHER TERESA

There is nothing small in the service of God.

~ST. FRANCIS OF SALES

The SOURCE of COURAGE and HOPE

*Give your worries to the LORD, and he will take care of
you. He will never let good people down.*

PSALM 55:22 NCV

Dedicated followers of Jesus may find their
courage tested by the inevitable anxieties and
fears that beset even the most courageous Christians.

When you find yourself worried about the challenges of today or the uncertainties of tomorrow, you
must ask yourself if you are ready to place your concerns and your life in God's all-powerful, all-knowing,
all-loving hands. If the answer to that question is yes—
as it should be—then you can draw courage and hope
from the source of strength that never fails: your heavenly Father.

> *Seeing that a Pilot steers the ship in which we sail, who will
> never allow us to perish even in the midst of shipwrecks, there
> is no reason why our minds should be overwhelmed with fear
> and overcome with weariness.*
>
> ~JOHN CALVIN

> *Just as courage is faith in good, so discouragement is faith in
> evil, and, while courage opens the door to good, discourage-
> ment opens it to evil.*
>
> ~HANNAH WHITALL SMITH

DEFEATING DISCOURAGEMENT

*The Lord himself will go before you. He will be with you; he will
not leave you or forget you. Don't be afraid and don't worry.*

DEUTERONOMY 31:8 NCV

When we fail to meet the expectations of others (or, for that matter, the expectations that we have set for ourselves), we may be tempted to abandon hope. Thankfully, on those cloudy days when our strength is sapped and our faith is shaken, there exists a source from which we can draw courage and wisdom. That source is God.

When we seek to form a more intimate and dynamic relationship with our Creator, He renews our spirits and restores our souls. God's promise is made clear in Isaiah 40:31: "But those who wait on the Lord shall renew their strength; they shall mount up with wings like eagles, they shall run and not be weary, they shall walk and not faint." And upon this promise we can—and should—depend.

*Faith and discouragement are opposites. Faith is taking God
at His Word no matter how bleak the circumstances appear to
be. Discouragement is focusing on distressing circumstances in
spite of what God has said. Learn to trust God.*

~JERRY FALWELL

Hope *for* Troubled Times

They won't be afraid of bad news; their hearts
are steady because they trust the Lord.

Psalm 112:7 ncv

These are troubled times, times when we have legitimate fears for the future of our nation, our world, and our families. We live in a fear-based world, a world where bad new travels at light speed and good news doesn't. But as Christians, we have every reason to live courageously. After all, the ultimate battle has already been fought and won on that faraway cross at Calvary.

Perhaps you, like countless other believers, have found your courage tested by the anxieties and fears that are an inevitable part of twenty-first-century life. If so, God wants to have a little chat with you. When you find your courage tested to the breaking point, God wants to remind you that He is not just near, He is here.

Your heavenly Father is your Protector and your Deliverer. Call upon Him in your hour of need, and be comforted. Whatever your challenge, whatever your trouble, God can certainly handle it. And will.

> *God shields us from most of the things we fear, but when He chooses not to shield us, He unfailingly allots grace in the measure needed.*
>
> ~Elisabeth Elliot

GREAT IS THY FAITHFULNESS

God is faithful, by whom you were called into the
fellowship of His Son, Jesus Christ our Lord.

1 CORINTHIANS 1:9

*A*s the hymn writer so eloquently wrote of God,
"Great is Thy faithfulness." God is faithful to
us even when we are not faithful to Him. God keeps
His promises to us even when we stray far from His
will. He continues to love us even when we disobey His
commandments. But God does not force His blessings
upon us. If we are to experience His love and His grace,
we must claim them for ourselves.

Are you tired, discouraged, or fearful? Be comforted:
God is with you. Are you confused? Listen to the quiet
voice of your heavenly Father. Are you bitter? Talk with
God and seek His guidance. Are you celebrating a great
victory? Thank God and praise Him. He is the Giver of
all things good. In whatever condition you find yourself, trust God and be comforted. The Father is with
you now and forever.

> *God's faithfulness has never depended on the faithfulness of*
> *his children. . . . God is greater than our weakness. In fact, I*
> *think, it is our weakness that reveals how great God is.*
>
> ~MAX LUCADO

To God Be *the* Glory

God is against the proud, but he gives grace to the humble.

1 Peter 5:5 NCV

*R*eality breeds humility. Dietrich Bonhoeffer observed, "It is very easy to overestimate the importance of our own achievements in comparison with what we owe others." And he was right.

As Christians, we have a profound reason to be humble: we have been refashioned and saved by Jesus Christ, and that salvation came not because of our own good works but because of God's grace. Thus, we are not "self-made," we are "God-made" and "Christ-saved." How then can we be boastful?

So, instead of puffing out your chest and saying, "Look how wonderful I am," give credit where credit is due, starting with God. And rest assured: There is no such thing as a self-made man or woman. All of us are made by God, and He deserves the glory, not us.

Without humility of heart all the other virtues by which one runs toward God seem—and are—absolutely worthless.

~Angela of Foligno

A humble heart is like a magnet that draws the favor of God toward us.

~Jim Cymbala

BEYOND ENVY

_Therefore, laying aside all malice, all deceit, hypocrisy,
envy, and all evil speaking, as newborn babes, desire the
pure milk of the word, that you may grow thereby._

1 PETER 2:1–2

od's Word warns us that envy is sin. Thus, we must guard ourselves against the natural tendency to feel resentment and jealousy when other people experience good fortune. As believers, we have absolutely no reason to be envious of any people on earth. After all, as Christians, we are already recipients of the greatest gift in all creation: God's grace. We have been promised the gift of eternal life through God's only begotten Son, and we must count that gift as our most precious possession.

So here's a simple suggestion that is guaranteed to bring you happiness: fill your heart with God's love, God's promises, and God's Son . . . and when you do, leave no room for envy, hatred, bitterness, or regret.

_How can you possess the miseries of envy when you possess in
Christ the best of all portions?_

~C. H. SPURGEON

_What God asks, does, or requires of others is not my business;
it is His._

~KAY ARTHUR

Living *in* Christ's Love

Yes, my dear children, live in him so that when Christ comes back, we can be without fear and not be ashamed in his presence. Since you know that Christ is righteous, you know that all who do right are God's children.

1 John 2:28–29 NCV

God's love for us is unconditional. No matter what we have done, good or bad, God's love is steady and sure. Even though we are imperfect, fallible human beings, even though we have fallen far short of God's commandments, Christ loves us still. His love is perfect; it does not waver, and it does not change. Our task, as believers, is to accept Christ's love and encourage others to do likewise.

In today's troubled world, we all need the love and peace that is found through the Son of God. Thankfully, Christ's love has no limits. We, in turn, should love Him with no limits, now and forever.

We are the earthen vessels, the jars of clay, that bring the life and love of Christ to one another.

~Sheila Walsh

The richest meaning of your life is contained in the idea that Christ loved you enough to give His life for you.

~Calvin Miller

YOU ARE PROTECTED

*The LORD himself will go before you. He will be with you; he will
not leave you or forget you. Don't be afraid and don't worry.*

DEUTERONOMY 31:8 NCV

he Bible makes this promise: God will care for you
and protect you. In Matthew 6, Jesus made this
point clear when He said, "Do not worry about your
life, what you will eat or what you will drink; nor about
your body, what you will put on. Is not life more than
food and the body more than clothing? Look at the birds
of the air, for they neither sow nor reap nor gather into
barns; yet your heavenly Father feeds them. Are you not
of more value than they? Which of you by worrying can
add one cubit to his stature? . . . Therefore do not worry
about tomorrow, for tomorrow will worry about its own
things. Sufficient for the day is its own trouble" (25–27,
34).

This beautiful passage reminds you that God still sits
in His heaven and you are His beloved child. Simply
put, you are protected.

*The Lord God of heaven and earth, the Almighty Creator of
all things, He who holds the universe in His hand as though
it were a very little thing, He is your Shepherd, and He has
charged Himself with the care and keeping of you, as a shepherd is charged with the care and keeping of his sheep.*

~HANNAH WHITALL SMITH

FACE-TO-FACE *with* OLD MAN TROUBLE

When you pass through the waters, I will be with you; and through the rivers, they shall not overflow you. When you walk through the fire, you shall not be burned, nor shall the flame scorch you. For I am the LORD your God, the Holy One of Israel, your Savior.

ISAIAH 43:2–3

As life unfolds, all of us encounter occasional setbacks; those occasional visits from Old Man Trouble are simply a fact of life, and none of us are exempt. When tough times arrive, we may be forced to rearrange our plans and our priorities. But even on our darkest days, we must remember that God's love remains constant.

The fact that we encounter adversity is not nearly as important as the way we choose to deal with it. When tough times arrive, we have a clear choice: we can begin the difficult work of tackling our troubles . . . or not. When we summon the courage to look Old Man Trouble squarely in the eye, an amazing thing usually happens: he blinks.

Faith is a strong power, mastering any difficulty in the strength of the Lord who made heaven and earth.

~CORRIE TEN BOOM

A Prescription *for* Panic

Anxiety in the heart of man causes depression,
but a good word makes it glad.

PROVERBS 12:25

We live in a world that sometimes seems to shift beneath our feet. We live in an uncertain world, a world where tragedies can befall even the most godly among us. And we are members of an anxious society, a society in which the changes we face threaten to outpace our abilities to make adjustments. No wonder we sometimes find ourselves beset by feelings of anxiety and panic.

At times, our anxieties may stem from physical causes—chemical imbalances in the brain that result in severe emotional distress or relentless panic attacks. In such cases, modern medicine offers hope to those who suffer. But oftentimes our anxieties result from spiritual deficits, not physical ones. And when we're spiritually depleted, the best prescription is found not in the medicine cabinet but deep inside the human heart. What we need is a higher daily dose of God's love, God's peace, God's assurance, and God's presence. And how do we acquire these blessings from our Creator? Through prayer, meditation, worship, and trust.

The thing that preserves a man from panic is his relationship to God.

~OSWALD CHAMBERS

A Sacrificial Love

"I am the good shepherd. The good shepherd gives His life for the sheep."

JOHN 10:11

Christ's love is perfect and steadfast. Even though we are fallible and wayward, the Shepherd cares for us still. Even though we have fallen far short of the Father's commandments, Christ loves us with a power and depth that is beyond our understanding. The sacrifice that Jesus made upon the cross was made for each of us, and His love endures to the edge of eternity and beyond.

Christ's love changes everything. When you accept His gift of grace, you are transformed, not only for today, but also for all eternity. If you haven't already done so, accept Jesus Christ as Your Savior. He's waiting patiently for you to invite Him into your heart. Please don't make Him wait a single minute longer.

This hard place in which you perhaps find yourself is the very place in which God is giving you opportunity to look only to Him, to spend time in prayer, and to learn long-suffering, gentleness, meekness—in short, to learn the depths of the love that Christ Himself has poured out on all of us.

~ELISABETH ELLIOT

Always Protected

*Be of good courage, and He shall strengthen your
heart, all you who hope in the LORD.*

PSALM 31:24

eing a courageous believer in this day and age is no easy task. Ours is a time of uncertainty and danger, a time when even the most courageous among us have legitimate cause for concern.

But here's the good news: if you've turned your heart and your life over to Jesus, you can live courageously, knowing that you have been saved by a loving Father and His only begotten Son.

Today, promise yourself that you will live without fear, knowing that even in these troubled times, God is always as near as your next breath—and you are always protected.

*God did away with all my fear. It was time for someone to
stand up—or in my case, sit down. So I refused to move.*

~ROSA PARKS

*A man who is intimate with God will never be intimidated
by men.*

~LEONARD RAVENHILL

Call upon God. Prayer itself can defuse fear.

~BILL HYBELS

FINDING ENCOURAGEMENT

*"Don't be afraid, because the LORD your God will
be with you everywhere you go."*

JOSHUA 1:9 NCV

*A*re you a hopeful, optimistic Christian who associates with like-minded people? If so, then you're both wise and blessed.

God offers us the strength to meet our challenges, and He offers us hope for the future. One way He shares His message of hope is through the words of encouraging friends and family members.

Hope is infectious: if we associate with hope-filled people, their enthusiasm will have a tendency to lift our spirits. But if we spend too much time in the company of negative people, our thoughts will tend to be detrimental.

So do yourself a favor and find people filled with hope. And spend time with them. When you catch their enthusiasm, share a little of that hope with those who need it.

> *I was learning something important: we are most vulnerable to the piercing winds of doubt when we distance ourselves from the mission and fellowship to which Christ has called us. Our night of discouragement will seem endless and our task impossible, unless we recognize that He stands in our midst.*
>
> ~JONI EARECKSON TADA

A Helping Hand

> *"But he who is greatest among you shall be your*
> *servant. And whoever exalts himself will be humbled,*
> *and he who humbles himself will be exalted."*
>
> MATTHEW 23:11–12

*I*f ever there was an example of generosity, it is Jesus. He lived generously, serving mankind, and He taught generosity.

He taught us that the most esteemed men and women are not the self-congratulatory leaders of society but are instead the humblest of servants. If you were being graded on generosity, how would you score? Would you earn As in philanthropy and humility? Hopefully so. But if your grades could stand a little improvement, this is the perfect day to begin.

Today, you may feel the urge to hoard your blessings. Don't do it. Instead, give generously to your neighbors, and do so without fanfare. Find a need and fill it . . . humbly. Lend a helping hand and share a word of kindness . . . anonymously. This is God's way.

The happiest and most joyful people are those who give money and serve.

~DAVE RAMSEY

A cheerful giver does not count the cost of what he gives. His heart is set on pleasing and cheering him to whom the gift is given.

~JULIANA OF NORWICH

Trust Him *to* Guide You

Trust the LORD with all your heart, and don't depend on your own understanding. Remember the LORD in all you do, and he will give you success.

PROVERBS 3:5–6 NCV

Christ has already fought and won our battle for us—He did so on the cross at Calvary. But despite Christ's sacrifice, and despite God's promises, we may become confused or disoriented by the endless complications and countless distractions.

If you're unsure of your next step, lean upon God's promises and lift your prayers to Him. Remember that God is your protector. Open yourself to His heart, and trust Him to guide you. When you do, God will direct your steps, and you will receive His blessings today, tomorrow, and throughout eternity.

> *It is a joy that God never abandons His children. He guides faithfully all who listen to His directions.*
>
> ~CORRIE TEN BOOM

> *God will prove to you how good and acceptable and perfect His will is when He's got His hands on the steering wheel of your life.*
>
> ~STUART AND JILL BRISCOE

HIS HEALING TOUCH

"I am the LORD who heals you."

EXODUS 15:26 NCV

God's Word has much to say about every aspect of your life, including your health. Are you concerned about your spiritual, physical, or emotional health? If so, there is a timeless source of comfort and assurance that is as near as your bookshelf. That source is the Holy Bible.

And when you face concerns of any sort—including health-related challenges—God is with You. So trust your medical doctor to do his or her part, but place your ultimate trust in your benevolent heavenly Father. His healing touch, like His love, endures forever.

Jesus Christ is the One by Whom, for Whom, through Whom everything was made. Therefore, He knows what's wrong in your life and how to fix it.

~ANNE GRAHAM LOTZ

Sometimes we get tired of the burdens of life, but we know that Jesus Christ will meet us at the end of life's journey. And that makes all the difference.

~BILLY GRAHAM

God Wants *to* Use You

*To everything there is a season, a time for every
purpose under heaven.*

ECCLESIASTES 3:1

God has things He wants you to do and places He wants you to go.

The most important decision of your life is your commitment to accept Jesus Christ as your personal Lord and Savior. And once your eternal destiny is secured, you will undoubtedly ask yourself the question, "What's next?" If you earnestly seek God's will for your life, you will find it . . . in time.

You may be certain that God is planning to use you in surprising, wonderful ways. And you may be certain that He intends to lead you along a path of His choosing. Your task is to watch for His signs, listen to His words, obey His commandments, and follow where He leads.

The place where God calls you is the place where your deep gladness and the world's deep hunger meet.

~FREDERICK BUECHNER

The only Person who has ever brought sustained power and purpose into my life is the living person of God. The only words that keep making sense are His words. The only way that always stands is His way.

~ANGELA THOMAS

CHRIST'S LOVE CHANGES EVERYTHING

Your old sinful self has died, and your new life is kept with Christ in God.

COLOSSIANS 3:3 NCV

What does the love of Christ mean to His believers? In a world where hope is in short supply, the love of Christ means everything. And Christ's love changes everything. His love is perfect and steadfast. Even though we are fallible and wayward, the Good Shepherd cares for us still. Even though we have fallen far short of the Father's commandments, Christ loves us with a power and depth that is beyond our understanding.

As we accept Christ's love and walk in Christ's footsteps, our lives bear testimony to His power and grace. Yes, Christ's love changes everything; may we invite Him into our hearts so it can then change everything in us.

There is not a single thing that Jesus cannot change, control, and conquer because He is the living Lord.

~FRANKLIN GRAHAM

I am Thine, O Lord; I have heard Thy voice, and it told Thy love to me. But I long to rise in the arms of faith and be closer drawn to Thee.

~FANNY CROSBY

Living Righteously

Flee also youthful lusts; but pursue righteousness, faith, love, peace with those who call on the Lord out of a pure heart.

2 Timothy 2:22

A life of righteousness is lived in accordance with God's commandments. A thoughtful believer strives to be faithful, honest, generous, disciplined, loving, kind, humble, and grateful, to name only a few of the more obvious qualities that are described in God's Word.

If we seek to follow the steps of Jesus, we must seek to live according to His teachings. In short, we must, to the best of our abilities, live according to the principles contained in the Holy Bible. When we do, we become powerful examples to our families and friends of the abundant hope that God bestows upon the righteous.

We are in desperate need for people of faith who are willing to courageously stand against sin and stand for righteousness.

~Susan Hunt

We must appropriate the tender mercy of God every day after conversion, or problems quickly develop. We need his grace daily in order to live a righteous life.

~Jim Cymbala

STRENGTH *for the* STRUGGLE

"My grace is sufficient for you, for My strength is made perfect in weakness."

2 CORINTHIANS 12:9

Has your faith been put to the test yet? If so, then you know that with God's help, you can endure life's darker days. And if you have not yet faced the inevitable trials and tragedies of life, you will.

Life is a tapestry of good days and difficult days, with good days predominating. During the good days, we are tempted to take our blessings for granted (a temptation that we must resist with all our might). But during life's difficult days, we discover precisely what we're made of. And more importantly, we discover what our faith is made of.

And when your faith is put to the test, rest assured that God is perfectly willing—and always ready—to give you strength for the struggle.

I believe that the Creator of this universe takes delight in turning the terrors and tragedies that come with living in this old, fallen domain of the devil and transforming them into something that strengthens our hope, tests our faith, and shows forth His glory.

~AL GREEN

HOPE *for an* ANXIOUS WORLD

*Be humble under God's powerful hand so he will
lift you up when the right time comes. Give all your
worries to him, because he cares about you.*

1 PETER 5:6–7 NCV

When calamity strikes anywhere in the world, we may be confronted with real-time images, images that breed anxiety. And as we stare transfixed at our television screens, we may fall prey to fear, discouragement, worry, or all three. But our Father in heaven has other plans. God has promised that we may lead lives of abundance, not anxiety. In fact, His Word instructs us to "be anxious for nothing" (Philippians 4:6). But how can we put our fears to rest? By taking those fears to God and leaving them there.

As you face the challenges of daily life, you may find yourself becoming anxious. If so, turn every one of your concerns over to your heavenly Father. The same God who created the universe will comfort you if you ask Him . . . so ask Him and trust Him. And then watch in amazement as your anxieties melt into the warmth of His loving hands.

One of the main missions of God is to free us from the debilitating bonds of fear and anxiety. God's heart is broken when He sees us so demoralized and weighed down by fear.

~BILL HYBELS

BORN AGAIN

You have been born again, and this new life did not come from something that dies, but from something that cannot die. You were born again through God's living message that continues forever.

1 PETER 1:23 NCV

Christ sacrificed His life so that we might be born again. This gift, freely given from God's only begotten Son, is the priceless possession of everyone who accepts Him as Lord and Savior.

Let us claim Christ's gift today. Let us walk with the Savior, let us love Him, let us praise Him, and let us share His message of salvation with all those who cross our paths.

The comforting words of Ephesians 2:8 make God's promise clear: "For by grace you have been saved through faith, and that not of yourselves; it is the gift of God." Thus, we are saved not because of our good deeds but because of our faith in Christ. May we, who have been given so much, praise our Savior for the gift of salvation, and may we share the joyous news of our Master's limitless love with our families, our friends, and the world.

Being born again is God's solution to our need for love and life and light.

~ANNE GRAHAM LOTZ

MIDCOURSE CORRECTIONS

*The wise see danger ahead and avoid it, but fools
keep going and get into trouble.*

PROVERBS 27:12 NCV

*A*re you facing one of life's inevitable "mid-course corrections"? If so, you must place your faith, your trust, and your life in the hands of the One who does not change: your heavenly Father.

In our fast-paced world, everyday life has become an exercise in managing change. Our circumstances change; our relationships change; our bodies change. We grow older every day, as does our world. Thankfully, God does not change. He is eternal, as are the truths found in His Holy Word.

He is the unmoving rock upon which you must construct this day and every day. When you do, you are secure.

We do not love each other without changing each other. We do not observe the world around us without in some way changing it, and being changed ourselves.

~MADELEINE L'ENGLE

Sometimes your medicine bottle says, "Shake well before using." That is what God has to do with some of his people. He has to shake them well before they are usable.

~VANCE HAVNER

COMFORTING OTHERS

Bear one another's burdens, and so fulfill the law of Christ.
GALATIANS 6:2

We live in a world that is, on occasion, a frightening place. Sometimes we sustain life-altering losses that are so profound and so tragic that it seems we could never recover. But with God's help and the help of encouraging family members and friends, we can recover.

In times of need, God's Word is clear: as believers, we must offer comfort to those in need by sharing not only our courage but also our faith. As the renowned revivalist Vance Havner observed, "No journey is complete that does not lead through some dark valleys. We can properly comfort others only with the comfort wherewith we ourselves have been comforted of God." Enough said.

So often we think that to be encouragers we have to produce great words of wisdom when, in fact, a few simple syllables of sympathy and an arm around the shoulder can often provide much needed comfort.

~FLORENCE LITTAUER

BEYOND *the* DIFFICULTIES

It will be hard when all these things happen to you. But after that you will come back to the LORD your God and obey him, because the LORD your God is a merciful God. He will not leave you or destroy you. He will not forget the Agreement with your ancestors, which he swore to them.

DEUTERONOMY 4:30–31 NCV

Sometimes the traffic jams, and sometimes the dog gobbles the homework. But when we find ourselves overtaken by the minor frustrations of life, we must catch ourselves, take a deep breath, and lift our thoughts upward. Although we are here on earth struggling to rise above the distractions of the day, we need never struggle alone. God is here—eternally and faithfully, with infinite patience and love—and if we reach out to Him, He will restore perspective and peace to our souls.

If you find yourself enduring difficult circumstances, remember that God remains in His heaven. If you become discouraged with the direction of your day or your life, lift your thoughts and prayers to Him. He will guide you through your difficulties and beyond them.

Whatever hallway you're in—no matter how long, how dark, or how scary—God is right there with you.

~BILL HYBELS

WRESTLING *with* OUR DOUBTS

Immediately the father of the child cried out and said with tears, "Lord, I believe; help my unbelief!"

MARK 9:24

ven the most faithful Christians are overcome by occasional bouts of uncertainty and doubt. You are no exception. You are a fallible human being, and just because you are a follower of Christ doesn't mean you will never experience times of doubt or fear.

When you feel that your faith is being tested to its limits, seek the comfort and assurance of the One who sent His Son as a sacrifice for you.

Even if you feel very distant from God, God is never distant from you. When you sincerely seek His presence, He will touch your heart, calm your fears, and restore your faith in the future . . . and your faith in Him.

> *We basically have two choices to make in dealing with the mysteries of God. We can wrestle with Him or we can rest in Him.*
>
> ~CALVIN MILLER

> *To wrestle with God does not mean that we have lost faith, but that we are fighting for it.*
>
> ~SHEILA WALSH

CALMING YOUR FEARS

"Do not be afraid; only believe."

MARK 5:36

We worry about the future and the past; we worry about finances and relationships. As we survey the landscape of our lives, we observe all manner of molehills and imagine them to be mountains. The irony is that most of the things we worry about will never come to pass, yet we worry still.

Are you concerned about the inevitable challenges that make up the fabric of everyday life? If so, why not ask God to help you regain a clear perspective about the problems and opportunities that confront you? When you petition your heavenly Father sincerely and seek His guidance, He can touch your heart, clear your vision, renew your mind, and calm your fears.

God alone can give us songs in the night.

~C. H. SPURGEON

I have found the perfect antidote for fear. Whenever it sticks up its ugly face, I clobber it with prayer.

~DALE EVANS ROGERS

In His Hands

*For whatever is born of God overcomes the world. And this is the
victory that has overcome the world—our faith.*

1 JOHN 5:4

The first element of a successful life is faith: faith in
God, faith in His Son, and faith in His promises. If
we place our lives in God's hands, our faith is rewarded
in ways that we—as human beings with clouded vision
and limited understanding—can scarcely comprehend.
But if we seek to rely solely upon our own resources,
or if we seek earthly success outside the boundaries
of God's commandments, we reap a bitter harvest for
ourselves and for our loved ones.

Do you desire the abundance and success that God
has promised? Then trust Him today and every day
that you live. Then, when you have entrusted your
future to the Giver of all things good, rest assured that
your future is secure, not only for today, but also for all
eternity.

*The Christian life is one of faith, where we find ourselves
routinely overdriving our headlights but knowing it's okay
because God is in control and has a purpose behind it.*

~BILL HYBELS

THE SHEPHERD'S CARE

God, your justice reaches to the skies. You have done great things; God, there is no one like you.

PSALM 71:19 NCV

It's a promise that is made over and over again in the Bible: whatever "it" is, God can handle it. When we're worried, God can reassure us; when we're sad, God can comfort us. When our hearts are broken, God is not just near, He is here. So we must lift our thoughts and prayers to Him. When we do, He will answer our prayers. Why? Because He is our shepherd, and He has promised to protect us now and forever.

Are you facing challenges that leave you fearful or discouraged? If so, you need not carry your burdens alone. God is ready to help, and the next move is yours.

Cast your cares on God; that anchor holds.

~ALFRED, LORD TENNYSON

When considering the size of your problems, there are two categories that you should never worry about: the problems that are small enough for you to handle, and the ones that aren't too big for God to handle.

~MARIE T. FREEMAN

God's Love

He who does not love does not know God, for God is love.

1 JOHN 4:8

God loves you. He loves you more than you can imagine; His affection is deeper than you can fathom. God made you in His own image and gave you salvation through the person of His Son, Jesus Christ. And as a result, you have an important decision to make. You must decide what to do about God's love: you can return it . . . or not.

When you accept the love that flows from the heart of God, you are transformed. When you embrace God's love, you feel differently about yourself, your neighbors, your community, your church, and your world. When you open your heart to God's love, you will feel compelled to share God's message and His compassion with others. God's heart is overflowing. Accept His love, return His love, and share His love. Today.

Our hearts have been made to cry out for a love that can come only from our Creator.

~ANGELA THOMAS

O the deep, deep love of Jesus, vast, unmeasured, boundless, and free; rolling as a mighty ocean in its fullness over me.

~SAMUEL TREVOR FRANCIS

A Simple Golden Rule

"Do to others what you want them to do to you."
MATTHEW 7:12 NCV

Would you like to make the world a better place? If so, you can start by practicing the Golden Rule.

Is the Golden Rule your rule, or is it just another Bible verse that goes in one ear and out the other? Jesus made Himself perfectly clear: He instructed you to treat other people in the same way that you want to be treated. But sometimes, especially when you're feeling the pressures of everyday living, obeying the Golden Rule can seem like an impossible task—but it's not. So if you want to know how to treat other people, ask the person you see every time you look into the mirror. The answer you receive will tell you exactly what to do.

> *It is one of the most beautiful compensations of life that no one can sincerely try to help another without helping herself.*
> ~BARBARA JOHNSON

> *It is wrong for anyone to be anxious to receive more from his neighbor than he himself is willing to give to God.*
> ~ST. FRANCIS OF ASSISI

A Shining Light

"While you have the light, believe in the light, that you may become sons of light." These things Jesus spoke, and departed, and was hidden from them.

JOHN 12:36

he Bible clearly states that you are "the light that gives light to the world" (Matthew 5:14 NCV). What kind of light have you been giving off lately? Hopefully you've been a good example for all to see. Why? Because the world needs all the light it can get, and that includes your light too.

Christ showed enduring love for you by willingly sacrificing His own life so that you might have eternal life. As a response to His sacrifice, you should love Him, praise Him, and share His message of salvation with your neighbors and with the world. So let your light shine today and every day. When you do, God will bless you now and forever.

You can't light another's path without casting light on your own.

~JOHN MAXWELL

Light is stronger than darkness—darkness cannot "comprehend" or "overcome" it.

~ANNE GRAHAM LOTZ

The LESSONS *of* TOUGH TIMES

I waited patiently for the LORD; and He
inclined to me, and heard my cry.

PSALM 40:1

Have you experienced a recent setback? If so, look for the lesson that God is trying to teach you. Instead of complaining about life's sad state of affairs, learn what needs to be learned, change what needs to be changed, and move on. View failure as an opportunity to reassess God's will for your life. And while you're at it, consider life's inevitable disappointments to be powerful opportunities to learn more—more about yourself, more about your circumstances, and more about your world.

Life can be difficult at times. And everybody, including you, makes mistakes. Your job is to make them only once. And how can you do that? By learning the lessons of tough times sooner rather than later, that's how.

God is able to take mistakes, when they are committed to Him,
and make of them something for our good and for His glory.
~RUTH BELL GRAHAM

Father, take our mistakes and turn them into opportunities.
~MAX LUCADO

GIVE ME PATIENCE, LORD, RIGHT NOW!

Now we exhort you, brethren, warn those who are unruly, comfort the fainthearted, uphold the weak, be patient with all.

1 THESSALONIANS 5:14

Most of us are impatient for God to grant us the desires of our heart. Usually we know what we want, and we know precisely when we want it: right now, if not sooner. But God may have other plans. And when God's plans differ from our own, we must trust in His infinite wisdom and His infinite love.

As busy men and women living in a fast-paced world, many of us find that waiting quietly for God is difficult. Why? Because we are fallible human beings seeking to live according to our own timetables, not God's. In our better moments, we realize that patience is not only a virtue, but also a commandment from God.

God instructs us to be patient in all things. We must be patient with our families, our friends, and our associates. We must also be patient with our Creator as He unfolds His plan for our lives. And that's as it should be. After all, think how patient God has been with us.

Our challenge is to wait in faith for the day of God's favor and salvation.

~JIM CYMBALA

Good Thinking

Be careful what you think, because your thoughts run your life.

PROVERBS 4:23 NCV

When you decided to allow Christ to rule over your heart, you entitled yourself to share in His promise of spiritual abundance and eternal joy. Have you claimed that entitlement? Are you an upbeat believer? Are you a person whose hopes and dreams are alive and well? Hopefully so. But sometimes, when pessimism and doubt invade your thoughts, you won't feel like celebrating. Why? Because thoughts are intensely powerful things.

You may need to spend more time thinking about your blessings, and less time fretting about your hardships. Then take time to thank the Giver of all things good for gifts that are, in truth, far too numerous to count.

> *As we have by faith said no to sin, so we should by faith say yes to God and set our minds on things above, where Christ is seated in the heavenlies.*
>
> ~VONETTE BRIGHT

> *Your thoughts are the determining factor as to whose mold you are conformed to. Control your thoughts and you control the direction of your life.*
>
> ~CHARLES STANLEY

ANSWERING OUR DOUBTS

For we do not want you to be ignorant, brethren, of our trouble which
came to us in Asia: that we were burdened beyond measure, above
strength, so that we despaired even of life. Yes, we had the sentence of
death in ourselves, that we should not trust in ourselves but in God who
raises the dead, who delivered us from so great a death, and does deliver
us; in whom we trust that He will still deliver us.

2 CORINTHIANS 1:8–10

When worries and doubts go unchecked, despair is soon to follow. Doubts come in several shapes and sizes: doubts about God, doubts about the future, and doubts about our own abilities, for starters. But when doubts creep in, as they will from time to time, we need not despair. As Sheila Walsh observed, "To wrestle with God does not mean that we have lost faith, but that we are fighting for it."

God never leaves our side, not for an instant. He is always with us, always willing to calm the storms of life. When we sincerely seek His presence—and when we genuinely seek to establish a deeper, more meaningful relationship with Him—God is prepared to touch our hearts, calm our fears, answer our doubts, and restore our confidence.

It is certainly wrong to despair. And if despair is wrong, hope is right.

~JOHN LUBBOCK

New Beginnings

"Do not remember the former things, nor consider the things of old. Behold, I will do a new thing."

Isaiah 43:18–19

Each new day offers countless opportunities to serve God, to seek His will, and to obey His teachings. But each day also offers countless opportunities to stray from God's commandments and to wander far from His path.

Sometimes we wander aimlessly in a wilderness of our own making, but God has better plans for us. And whenever we ask Him to renew our strength and guide our steps, He does so.

Consider this day a new beginning. Consider it a fresh start, a renewed opportunity to serve your Creator with willing hands and a loving heart. Ask God to renew your sense of purpose as He guides your steps. Today is a glorious opportunity to serve your Father in heaven. Seize that opportunity while you can because tomorrow might be too late.

If the leaves had not been let go to fall and wither, if the tree had not consented to be a skeleton for many months, there would be no new life rising, no bud, no flower, no fruit, no seed, no new generation.

~Elisabeth Elliot

GOD IS HERE

—⚯—

Come near to God, and God will come near to you.

JAMES 4:8 NCV

*A*s you think about the day ahead, here's an important question to ask yourself: "Do I expect God to walk with me every step of the way?" The answer to that question has nothing to do with God and everything to do with you. God will most certainly be there for you. Will you be there with Him?

When you begin the day with prayer and praise, God often seems very near indeed. But if you ignore God's presence or—worse yet—rebel against it altogether, the world in which you live becomes a spiritual wasteland.

The comforting words of Psalm 46:10 remind us to "be still, and know that I am God." When we do, we sense the loving presence of our heavenly Father, and we are comforted by the certain knowledge that God is not far away . . . and He isn't even nearby. He is, quite literally, here. And it's up to each of us to sense His presence.

The things God delights in, kindness, justice, and righteousness, are the essence of Christianity. If he delights in these things, then his followers must also.

~MARY MORRISON SUGGS

WORDS *of* HOPE

*Wise people's minds tell them what to say, and
that helps them be better teachers.*

PROVERBS 16:23 NCV

God's Word reminds us that "careless words stab like a sword, but wise words bring healing" (Proverbs 12:18 NCV). If you seek to be a source of encouragement to friends, family members, and coworkers, then you must measure your words carefully. And that's exactly what God wants you to do.

Today, make this promise to yourself: vow to be an honest, effective, encouraging communicator at work, home, and everyplace in between. Speak wisely, not impulsively. Use words of kindness and praise, not words of anger or derision. Learn how to be truthful without being cruel. Remember that you have the power to heal others or injure them, to lift others up or hold them back. And when you learn how to lift them up, you'll soon discover that you've lifted yourself up too.

Attitude and the spirit in which we communicate are as important as the words we say.

~CHARLES STANLEY

Keeping the lines of communication open can help exterminate the pests that gnaw away at love.

~ANNIE CHAPMAN

The POWER *of* FAITH

Have faith in the LORD your God, and you will stand strong.
Have faith in his prophets, and you will succeed.

2 CHRONICLES 20:20 NCV

*L*ife is a series of successes and failures, celebrations and disappointments, joys and sorrows. God stands beside you every step of the way, through every triumph and tragedy, strengthening you if you have faith in Him. Jesus taught His disciples that if they had faith, they could move mountains. You can too.

When you place your faith, your trust, indeed your very life, in the hands of Christ Jesus, you'll be amazed at what He can do with you and through you. As you trust God's plans, your faith will be strengthened through praise, worship, Bible study, and prayer. With Him, all things are possible! Just imagine the marvelous world of possibilities that will open to you if you have faith.

O holy Savior, Friend unseen, the faint, the weak on Thee may lean, help me, throughout life's varying scene, by faith to cling to Thee.

~CHARLOTTE ELLIOTT

Let your faith in Christ be in the quiet confidence that He will, every day and every moment, give you the strength you need.

~ANDREW MURRAY

Solving *the* Riddles

But if any of you needs wisdom, you should ask God for it. He is generous to everyone and will give you wisdom without criticizing you.

JAMES 1:5 NCV

*A*re you facing a difficult decision? Take your concerns to God and avail yourself of the messages and mentors that He has placed along your path. Life presents each of us with countless questions, conundrums, doubts, and problems.

Thankfully, the riddles of everyday living are not too difficult to solve if we look for answers in the right places. When we have questions, we should consult God's Word, we should seek the guidance of the Holy Spirit, and we should trust the counsel of God-fearing friends and family members.

When you do, God will speak to you in His own way and in His own time, and when He does, you can most certainly trust the answers He gives.

As we trust God to give us wisdom for today's decisions, He will lead us a step at a time into what He wants us to be doing in the future.

~THEODORE EPP

Be to the world a sign that while we as Christians do not have all the answers, we do know and care about the questions.

~BILLY GRAHAM

LIFE ETERNAL

"In a little while the world will not see me anymore, but you will see me. Because I live, you will live, too."

JOHN 14:19 NCV

Ours is a God who understands, far better than we ever could, the essence of what it means to be human. How marvelous it is that God became a man and walked among us. Had He not chosen to do so, we might feel removed from a distant Creator. But ours is not a distant God.

God understands our hopes, our fears, and our temptations. He understands what it means to be angry and what it costs to forgive. He knows the heart, the conscience, and the soul of every person who has ever lived, including you. And God has a plan of salvation that is intended for you. Accept it. Accept God's gift through the person of His Son, Christ Jesus, and then rest assured: God walked among us so that you might have eternal life. Amazing though it may seem, He did it for you.

If you are a believer, your judgment will not determine your eternal destiny. Christ's finished work on Calvary was applied to you the moment you accepted Christ as Savior.

~BETH MOORE

On BEYOND FAILURE

There is a time for everything, and everything on earth has its special season. . . . There is a time to cry and a time to laugh. There is a time to be sad and a time to dance.

ECCLESIASTES 3:1, 4 NCV

The occasional disappointments and failures of life are inevitable; there is simply no way around it. You will experience your fair share of setbacks that are simply the price you must occasionally pay for your willingness to take risks as you follow your dreams. But even when you encounter bitter disappointments, you must never lose hope.

Whenever we encounter the difficulties of life, God stands ready to protect us. Our responsibility is to ask Him for protection. When we call upon Him in heartfelt prayer, He will answer—in His own time and according to His own plan—and He will heal us. And while we are waiting for God's plans to unfold and for His healing touch to restore us, we can be comforted in the knowledge that our Creator can overcome any obstacle, even if we cannot.

Every misfortune, every failure, every loss may be transformed. God has the power to transform all misfortunes into "God-sends."

~MRS. CHARLES E. COWMAN

The Last Word

For God has not given us a spirit of fear, but of
power and of love and of a sound mind.

2 Timothy 1:7

*A*ll of us may find our courage tested by the inevitable disappointments and tragedies of life. After all, ours is a world filled with uncertainty, hardship, sickness, and danger. Trouble, it seems, is never too far from the front door.

When we focus on our fears and our doubts, we may find many reasons to lie awake at night and fret about the uncertainties of the coming day. A better strategy is to focus not upon our fears but instead upon our God.

God is your shield and your strength; you are His forever. So don't focus your thoughts on the fears of the day. Instead, trust God's plan and His eternal love for you. And remember: God is good, and He has the last word.

> *Fear is a self-imposed prison that will keep you from becoming what God intends for you to be.*
>
> ~Rick Warren

> *Only believe, don't fear. Our Master, Jesus, always watches over us, and no matter what the persecution, Jesus will surely overcome it.*
>
> ~Lottie Moon

In the FOOTSTEPS *of* JESUS

Whoever serves me must follow me. Then my servant will be with
me everywhere I am. My Father will honor anyone who serves me.

JOHN 12:26 NCV

ho will you walk with today? Will you walk with
people who worship the ways of the world? Or
will you walk with the Son of God? Jesus walks with
you. Are you walking with Him? Hopefully you will
choose to walk with Him today and every day of your
life. God's Word promises that when you follow in
Christ's footsteps, you will learn how to live freely and
lightly (Matthew 11:28–30).

If we are to be disciples of Christ, we must trust Him
and place Him at very center of our beings. Jesus never
comes "next." He is always first. The wonderful para-
dox is that it is only by sacrificing ourselves to Him that
we gain eternal salvation. Do you seek to fulfill God's
purpose for your life? Then follow Christ. Follow Him
by picking up His cross today and every day that you
live. Then you will quickly discover that Christ's love
has the power to change everything, including you.

A disciple is a follower of Christ. That means you take on His
priorities as your own. His agenda becomes your agenda. His
mission becomes your mission.

~CHARLES STANLEY

GOD IS LOVE

And we have known and believed the love that God has for us. God is love, and he who abides in love abides in God, and God in him.

1 JOHN 4:16

The Bible makes this promise: God is love. It's a sweeping statement, a profoundly important description of what God is and how God works. God's love is perfect. When we open our hearts to His perfect love, we are touched by the Creator's hand, and we are transformed.

Today, even if you can only carve out a few quiet moments, offer sincere prayers of thanksgiving to your Creator. He loves you now and throughout all eternity. Open your heart to His presence and His love.

The life of faith is a daily exploration of the constant and countless ways in which God's grace and love are experienced.
~EUGENE PETERSON

Joy is the heart's harmonious response to the Lord's song of love.

~A. W. TOZER

TRANSCENDENT LOVE

Who shall separate us from the love of Christ? Shall tribulation, or distress, or persecution, or famine, or nakedness, or peril, or sword? . . . Yet in all these things we are more than conquerors through Him who loved us.

ROMANS 8:35, 37

Where can we find God's love? Everywhere. God's love transcends space and time. It reaches beyond the heavens, and it touches the darkest, smallest corner of every human heart. When we become passionate in our devotion to the Father, when we sincerely open our minds and hearts to Him, His love does not arrive "some day"—it arrives immediately.

Today, take God at His word and welcome His Son into your heart. When you do, God's transcendent love will surround you and transform you, now and forever.

The grace of God transcends all our feeble efforts to describe it. It cannot be poured into any mental receptacle without running over.

~VANCE HAVNER

Praise the Father for his loving kindness; tenderly cares He for His erring children. Praise Him.

~ELIZABETH R. CHARLES

INFINITE POSSIBILITIES

"Is anything too hard for the LORD?"

GENESIS 18:14

Ours is a God of infinite possibilities. But sometimes, because of limited faith and limited understanding, we wrongly assume that God cannot or will not intervene in the affairs of mankind. Such assumptions are simply wrong.

Are you afraid to ask God to do big things in your life? Is your faith threadbare and worn? If so, it's time to abandon your doubts and reclaim your faith in God's promises.

God's Holy Word makes it clear: absolutely nothing is impossible for the Lord. And since the Bible means what it says, you can be comforted in the knowledge that the Creator of the universe can do miraculous things in your own life and in the lives of your loved ones. Your challenge, as a believer, is to take God at His word, and to expect the miraculous.

> *We will see more and more that we are chosen not because of our ability, but because of the Lord's power, which will be demonstrated in our not being able.*
>
> ~CORRIE TEN BOOM

> *So God's patience is His power over Himself. Great is that God who, having all power, yet keeps all power subject to Himself.*
>
> ~JIM ELLIOT

HOPE IS CONTAGIOUS

Finally, all of you be of one mind, having compassion for one another; love as brothers, be tenderhearted, be courteous.

1 PETER 3:8

One of the reasons that God placed you here on earth is so that you might become a beacon of encouragement to the world. As a faithful follower of the One from Galilee, you have every reason to be hopeful, and you have every reason to share your hopes with others. When you do, you will discover that hope, like other human emotions, is contagious.

As a follower of Christ, you are instructed to choose your words carefully so as to build others up through wholesome, honest encouragement (Ephesians 4:29). So look for the good in others and celebrate the good that you find. As the old saying goes, "When someone does something good, applaud—you'll make two people happy."

> *One of the ways God refills us after failure is through the blessing of Christian fellowship. Just experiencing the joy of simple activities shared with other children of God can have a healing effect on us.*
>
> ~ANNE GRAHAM LOTZ

HELPING NEIGHBORS *in* NEED

*Let each of us please his neighbor for his good,
leading to edification.*

ROMANS 15:2

Who are our neighbors? Jesus answered that question with the story of the good Samaritan. Our neighbors are any people whom God places in our paths, especially those in need.

We know that we are instructed to love our neighbors, and yet there's so little time and we're so busy. No matter. As Christians, we are commanded by our Lord and Savior to love our neighbors just as we love ourselves. Period.

This very day you will encounter someone who needs a word of encouragement, or a pat on the back, or a helping hand, or a heartfelt prayer. And if you don't reach out to that person, who will? If you don't take the time to understand the needs of your neighbors, who will? If you don't love your brothers and sisters, who will? So, today, look for a neighbor in need, and then do something to help. Father's orders.

The truest help we can render an afflicted man is not to take his burden from him, but to call out his best energy, that he may be able to bear the burden himself.

~PHILLIPS BROOKS

His Voice

*"Fear not, for I am with you; be not dismayed, for I am
your God. I will strengthen you, yes, I will help you, I
will uphold you with My righteous right hand."*

ISAIAH 41:10

Sometimes God speaks loudly and clearly. More
often, He speaks in a quiet voice—and if you are
wise, you will be listening carefully when He does. To
do so, you must carve out quiet moments each day to
study His Word and sense His direction.

Can you quiet yourself long enough to listen to your
conscience? Are you attuned to the subtle guidance of
your intuition? Are you willing to pray sincerely and
then wait quietly for God's response? Hopefully so.
Usually God refrains from sending His messages on
stone tablets or city billboards. More often He commu-
nicates in subtler ways. If you sincerely desire to hear
His voice, you must listen carefully, and you must do so
in the silent corners of your quiet, willing heart.

*Half an hour of listening is essential except when one is very
busy. Then, a full hour is needed.*

~St. Francis of Sales

HE RENEWS OUR STRENGTH

Have you not known? Have you not heard? The everlasting God, the LORD, the Creator of the ends of the earth, neither faints nor is weary. His understanding is unsearchable. He gives power to the weak, and to those who have no might He increases strength.

ISAIAH 40:28–29

Are you almost too weary to lift your head? Then bow it. When we genuinely lift our hearts and prayers to God, He renews our strength. Offer your concerns and fears to your Father in heaven. He is always at your side, offering His love and His strength.

Are you troubled or anxious? Take your anxieties to God in prayer. Are you weak or worried? Delve deeply into God's Holy Word and sense His presence in the quiet moments of the day. Are you spiritually exhausted? Call upon fellow believers to support you, and call upon Christ to renew your spirit and your life. Your Savior will never let you down. To the contrary, He will always lift you up if you ask Him to. So what, dear friend, are you waiting for?

God is not running an antique shop! He is making all things new!

~VANCE HAVNER

He is the God of wholeness and restoration.

~STORMIE OMARTIAN

A Time *to* Rest

"Come to Me, all you who labor and are heavy laden, and I will give you rest. Take My yoke upon you and learn from Me, for I am gentle and lowly in heart, and you will find rest for your souls. For My yoke is easy and My burden is light."

MATTHEW 11:28–30

God expects us to work hard, but He also intends for us to rest. When we fail to take the rest we need, we do a disservice to ourselves and our families. Sometimes the struggles of life can drain us of our strength.

When we find ourselves tired, discouraged, or worse, there is a source from which we can draw the power needed to recharge our spiritual batteries. That source is God.

Is your spiritual battery running low? Is your energy on the wane? Are your emotions frayed? If so, it's time to turn your thoughts and your prayers to God. And when you're finished, it's time to rest.

If we stay with the Lord, enduring to the end of His great plan for us, we will enjoy the rest that results from living in the kingdom of God.

~SERITA ANN JAKES

The GIFT of TODAY

_This is the day that the LORD has made.
Let us rejoice and be glad today!_

PSALM 118:24 NCV

For Christians, every day begins and ends with God and His Son. Christ came to this earth to give us abundant life and eternal salvation. We give thanks to our Maker when we treasure each day and use it to the fullest.

Today is God's gift to you. How you use it is your gift to God. So how do you plan to use today's gift? Will you celebrate God's blessings and obey His commandments? Will you share words of encouragement and hope with all who cross your path? Will you share the good news of the risen Christ? Only you can answer these questions. May you answer wisely today and every day of your life.

With each new dawn, life delivers a package to your front door, rings your doorbell, and runs.

~CHARLES SWINDOLL

Today is mine. Tomorrow is none of my business. If I peer anxiously into the fog of the future, I will strain my spiritual eyes so that I will not see clearly what is required of me now.

~ELISABETH ELLIOT

Our Ultimate Hope

And we have seen and testify that the Father has
sent the Son as Savior of the world.

1 John 4:14

hrist is the ultimate Savior of mankind and the personal hope of those who believe in Him. Thomas Brooks spoke for believers of every generation when he observed, "Christ is the sun, and all the watches of our lives should be set by the dial of his motion." As His servants, we should place Him at the very center of our lives. And every day that God gives us breath, we should share Christ's love and His message with a world that needs both.

Christ is no Moses, no exactor, no giver of laws, but a giver of grace, a Savior; he is infinite mercy and goodness, freely and bountifully given to us.

~Martin Luther

I now know the power of the risen Lord! He lives! The dawn of Easter has broken in my own soul! My night is gone!

~Mrs. Charles E. Cowman

Jesus be mine forever, my God, my heaven, my all.

~C. H. Spurgeon

GROWING WISE

You are my hope, O Lord GOD; You are my trust from my youth.

*W*isdom and hope are traveling companions. Wise men and women learn to think optimistically about their lives, their futures, and their faith. The pessimists, however, are not so fortunate; they choose instead to focus their thoughts and energies on fault-finding, criticizing, and complaining, with precious little to show for their efforts.

To become wise, we must seek God's wisdom—the wisdom of hope—and we must live according to God's Word. To become wise, we must seek God's guidance with consistency and purpose. To become wise, we must not only learn the lessons of life, we must live by them.

Do you seek wisdom for yourself and for your family? Then remember this: the ultimate source of wisdom is the Word of God. When you study God's Word and live according to His commandments, you will grow wise, you will remain hopeful, and you will be a blessing to your family and to the world.

> *Wisdom is knowledge applied. Head knowledge is useless on the battlefield. Knowledge stamped on the heart makes one wise.*
>
> ~BETH MOORE

LIVING *on* PURPOSE

Whatever you do, do all to the glory of God.
1 CORINTHIANS 10:31

*L*ife is best lived on purpose. And purpose, like everything else in the universe, begins with God. Whether you realize it or not, God has a plan for your life, a divine calling, a direction in which He is leading you. When you welcome God into your heart and establish a genuine relationship with Him, He will begin, in time, to make His purposes known.

Sometimes God's intentions will be clear to you; other times God's plan will seem uncertain, at best. But even on those difficult days when you are unsure which way to turn, you must never lose sight of these overriding facts: God created you for a reason, He has important work for you to do, and He's waiting patiently for you to do it.

And the next step is up to you.

> *If the Lord calls you, He will equip you for the task He wants you to fulfill.*
>
> ~WARREN WIERSBE

> *There is a path before you that you alone can walk. There is a purpose that you alone can fulfill.*
>
> ~KARLA DORNACHER

Friends *and* Family

As iron sharpens iron, so people can improve each other.
PROVERBS 27:17 NCV

We can give thanks to our generous heavenly Father for many things, but a loving family is a treasure from God, and so is a trustworthy friend. If you are a member of a close-knit, supportive family, offer a word of thanks to your Creator. And if you have a close circle of trustworthy friends, consider yourself richly blessed.

Today, take time to praise God for your family and your friends. God has placed these people along your path—love them and care for them. These people are, in a very real sense, gifts from God; we should treat them as such.

> *The best times in life are made a thousand times better when shared with a dear friend.*
>
> ~LUCI SWINDOLL

> *God often keeps us on the path by guiding us through the counsel of friends and trusted spiritual advisors.*
>
> ~BILL HYBELS

DECISION-MAKING 101

Such doubters are thinking two different things at the same time, and they cannot decide about anything they do. They should not think they will receive anything from the Lord.

JAMES 1:8 NCV

ecisions! Decisions! Decisions! All day long you must make decisions—decisions about the things you do, decisions about the words you speak, and decisions about the thoughts you choose to think.

If you're facing one of life's major decisions, here are some things you can do: (1) Gather as much information as you can. (2) Don't be too impulsive. (3) Rely on the advice of trusted friends and mentors. (4) Pray for guidance. (5) Trust the quiet inner voice of your conscience. (6) When the time for action arrives, act. Procrastination is the enemy of progress; don't let it defeat you.

People who can never quite seem to make up their minds usually make themselves miserable. So when in doubt, be decisive. It's the decent way to live.

> *There is no need to fear the decisions of life when you know Jesus Christ, for His name is Counselor.*
>
> ~WARREN WIERSBE

> *No trumpets sound when the important decisions of our life are made. Destiny is made known silently.*
>
> ~AGNES DEMILLE

Filled with the Spirit

Do not be drunk with wine, which will ruin you,
but be filled with the Spirit.

EPHESIANS 5:18 NCV

*A*re you burdened by the pressures of everyday living? If so, it's time to take the pressure off. How can you do that? By allowing the Holy Spirit to fill you and do His work in your life.

When you are filled with the Holy Spirit, your words and deeds will reflect a love and devotion to Christ. When you are filled with the Holy Spirit, the steps of your life's journey are guided by the Lord. When you allow God's Spirit to work in you and through you, you will be energized and transformed.

Today, allow yourself to be filled with the Spirit of God. And then stand back in amazement as God begins to work miracles in your own life and in the lives of those you love.

> *Whether we preach, pray, write, do business, travel, take care of children, or administer the government—whatever we do—our whole life and influence should be filled with the power of the Holy Spirit.*
>
> ~CHARLES FINNEY

> *The Holy Spirit is like a living and continually flowing fountain in believers. We have the boundless privilege of tapping into that fountain every time we pray.*
>
> ~SHIRLEY DOBSON

The PROMISE *of* STRENGTH

But may the God of all grace, who called us to His
eternal glory by Christ Jesus, after you have suffered a
while, perfect, establish, strengthen, and settle you.

1 PETER 5:10

od promises us eternal life through His Son, Jesus Christ, but God does not promise us that our earthly lives will be free from suffering. Instead, He promises that He will give comfort to the suffering, strength to the weary, and healing to those who grieve. God promises that wherever we are, whether at the peak of the mountaintop or in the darkness of the deepest valley, He will be with us always . . . and that promise, dear friends, is always enough.

> *Part of every misery is, so to speak, the misery's shadow or*
> *reflection: the fact that you don't merely suffer but that you*
> *have to keep on thinking about the fact that you suffer. I not*
> *only live each endless day in grief, but I live each day thinking*
> *about living each day in grief.*
>
> ~C. S. LEWIS

> *The love of God exists in its strongest and purest form in the*
> *very midst of suffering and tragedy.*
>
> ~SUZANNE DALE EZELL

How We Thank Him

We always thank God, the Father of our Lord Jesus Christ.
COLOSSIANS 1:3 NCV

*H*ow do we thank God for the gifts He has given us? By using those gifts for the glory of His kingdom.

God has given you talents and opportunities that are uniquely yours. Are you willing to use your gifts in the way that God intends? And are you willing to summon the discipline that is required to develop your talents and hone your skills? That's precisely what God wants you to do, and that's precisely what you should desire for yourself.

As you seek to expand your talents, you will undoubtedly encounter stumbling blocks along the way, such as the fear of rejection or the fear of failure. When you do, don't stumble! Just continue to refine your skills, and offer your services to God. And when the time is right, He will use you. But it's up to you to be thoroughly prepared when He does.

> *One thing taught large in the Holy Scriptures is that while God gives His gifts freely, He will require a strict accounting of them at the end of the road. Each man is personally responsible for his store, be it large or small, and will be required to explain his use of it before the judgment seat of Christ.*
> ~A. W. TOZER

HIS TRANSFORMING POWER

Your old sinful self has died, and your new life is
kept with Christ in God.

COLOSSIANS 3:3 NCV

Righteous believers who fashion their days around Jesus see the world differently; they act differently, and they feel differently about themselves and their neighbors. Hopefully you too will be such a believer. God's hand has the power to transform your day and your life. Your task is to accept Christ's grace with a humble, thankful heart as you receive the "new life" that can be yours through Him.

Do you desire to improve some aspect of your life? If so, don't expect changing circumstances to miraculously transform you into the person you want to become. Transformation starts with God, and it starts in the quiet corners of a willing human heart—like yours.

God's work is not in buildings, but in transformed lives.
~RUTH BELL GRAHAM

God's omniscience can instill you with a supernatural confidence that can transform your life.
~BILL HYBELS

A Book Unlike Any Other

For I am not ashamed of the gospel of Christ, for it is the power of God to salvation for everyone who believes.

The Bible is a priceless gift, a tool for Christians to use as they share the good news of their Savior, Christ Jesus. Too many Christians, however, keep their spiritual tool kits tightly closed and out of sight, with predictably unfortunate results.

God's Word is unlike any other book. A. W. Tozer wrote, "The purpose of the Bible is to bring men to Christ, to make them holy and prepare them for heaven. In this it is unique among books, and it always fulfills its purpose."

George Mueller observed, "The vigor of our spiritual lives will be in exact proportion to the place held by the Bible in our lives and in our thoughts." As Christians, we are called upon to study God's Holy Word and then share it with the world.

God's Holy Word is, indeed, a priceless, one-of-a-kind treasure. Handle it with care, but, more importantly, handle it every day.

> *Unless we form the habit of going to the Bible in bright moments as well as in trouble, we cannot fully respond to its consolations because we lack equilibrium between light and darkness.*
> ~HELEN KELLER

ABOVE *and* BEYOND OUR CIRCUMSTANCES

Should we take only good things from God and not trouble?

JOB 2:10 NCV

ven the most devout Christians can become discouraged, and you are no exception. After all, you live in a world where expectations can be high and demands can be even higher.

If you find yourself enduring difficult circumstances, don't lose hope. If you face uncertainties about the future, don't become anxious. And if you become discouraged with the direction of your day or your life, don't despair. Instead, lift your thoughts and prayers to your heavenly Father. He is a God of possibility, not negativity. You can be sure that He will guide you through your difficulties and beyond them . . . far beyond.

> *When you realize that your circumstances, no matter how overwhelming or pressing, are ruled by a King who seeks your highest good, you can truly "consider it all joy when you fall into various trials, knowing that the testing of your faith produces patience . . . that you may be perfect and complete, lacking in nothing" (James 1:2–4).*
>
> ~CHARLES SWINDOLL

A Light *on the* Path

Your word is a lamp to my feet and a light to my path.

PSALM 119:105

The psalmist describes God's word as "a light to my path." Is the Bible your lamp? If not, you are depriving yourself of a priceless gift from the Creator.

Are you a person who trusts God's Word without reservation? Hopefully so, because the Bible is unlike any other book—it is a guidebook for life here on earth and for life eternal.

Vance Havner observed, "It takes calm, thoughtful, prayerful meditation on the Word to extract its deepest nourishment." How true. God's Word can be a road-map to a place of righteous and abundance. Make it your roadmap. God's wisdom can be a light to guide your steps. Claim it as your light today, tomorrow, and every day of your life—and then walk confidently in the footsteps of God's only begotten Son.

> *Our nighttime passage through the dark and dangerous journey of this life is illuminated by God's Word, the Bible: "Your word is a lamp to my feet and light for my path." It is a light for our darkness and for our brighter times as well.*
>
> ~James Montgomery Boice

Dream Big

With God's power working in us, God can do much, much more than anything we can ask or imagine.

EPHESIANS 3:20 NCV

Your heavenly Father created you with unique gifts and untapped talents; your job is to tap into them. When you do, you'll begin to feel an increasing sense of confidence in yourself and in your future.

Are you willing to entertain the possibility that God has big plans in store for you? Hopefully so. Yet sometimes, especially if you've recently experienced a life-altering disappointment, you may find it difficult to envision a brighter future for yourself and your family. If so, it's time to reconsider your own capabilities . . . and God's.

So even if you're experiencing difficult days, don't abandon your dreams. Instead, trust that God is preparing you for greater things.

When you affirm big, believe big, and pray big, big things happen.

~NORMAN VINCENT PEALE

You pay God a compliment by asking great things of Him.

~ST. TERESA OF AVILA

Good Pressures, Bad Pressures

Do you think I am trying to make people accept me? No, God is the One I am trying to please. Am I trying to please people? If I still wanted to please people, I would not be a servant of Christ.

GALATIANS 1:10 NCV

Our world is filled with pressures: some good, some bad. The pressures that we feel to follow God's will and obey His commandments are positive pressures. God places them on our hearts, and He intends that we act in accordance with His leadings. But we also face different pressures, ones that are definitely not from God. When we feel pressured to do things—or even to think thoughts—that lead us away from God, we must beware.

Society seeks to mold us into more worldly beings; God seeks to mold us into new beings that are most certainly not conformed to this world. If we are to please God, we must resist the pressures that society seeks to impose upon us, and we must conform ourselves, instead, to God's will, to His path, and to His Son.

I have found that the closer I am to the godly people around me, the easier it is for me to live a righteous life because they hold me accountable.

~JOHN MACARTHUR

STANDING UP *for* YOUR FAITH

Watch, stand fast in the faith, be brave, be strong.

1 CORINTHIANS 16:13

Genuine faith is never meant to be locked up in the heart of a believer; to the contrary, it is meant to be shared with the world. But if you sincerely seek to share your faith, you must first find it.

Every life—including yours—is marked by success and failure, celebration and disappointment, joy and sorrow. During these peaks and valleys, you must remember that God is standing by your side at every step, through every triumph and tragedy. God will give you strength if you simply have faith in Him.

As your faith grows and becomes stronger, you will find ways to share it with your friends, your family, and the world. You will be astounded at the wonderful things Christ Jesus can do with you and through you when you simply put your life in His hands. God makes all things possible when you trust Him. He stands ready to open a world of endless opportunities and possibilities to you if you have faith.

> *Talk faith. The world is better off without your uttered ignorance and morbid doubt. If you have faith in God, or man, or self, say so. If not, push back upon the shelf of silence all your thoughts, till faith shall come; no one will grieve because your lips are dumb.*
>
> ~ELLA WHEELER WILCOX

A Passion *for* Life

But those who wait on the LORD shall renew their strength;
they shall mount up with wings like eagles, they shall run
and not be weary, they shall walk and not faint.

ISAIAH 40:31

*I*f your enthusiasm for life has waned, it is now
time to redirect your efforts and recharge your
spiritual batteries. And that means refocusing your priorities by putting God first and counting your blessings
instead of your troubles.

Nothing is more important than your wholehearted
commitment to your Creator and to His only begotten
Son. Your faith must never be an afterthought; it must
be your ultimate priority, your ultimate possession,
and your ultimate passion. When you become passionate about your faith, you'll become passionate about
your life too. And God will smile.

Don't take hold of a thing unless you want that thing to take
hold of you.

~E. STANLEY JONES

If your heart has grown cold, it is because you have moved
away from the fire of His presence.

~BETH MOORE

RELYING *Upon* HIM

*Be humble under God's powerful hand so he will
lift you up when the right time comes. Give all your
worries to him, because he cares about you.*

1 PETER 5:6–7 NCV

*D*o the demands of this day threaten to overwhelm you? If so, you must rely not only upon your own resources but also upon the promises of your Father in heaven. God is a never-ending source of support and courage for those of us who call upon Him. When we are weary, He gives us strength. When we see no hope, God reminds us of His promises. When we grieve, God wipes away our tears.

God will hold your hand and walk with you every day of your life if you let Him. So even if your circumstances are difficult, trust the Father. His love is eternal and His goodness endures forever.

*Snuggle in God's arms. When you are hurting, when you feel
lonely or left out, let Him cradle you, comfort you, reassure
you of His all-sufficient power and love.*

~KAY ARTHUR

*Whatever may be our circumstances in life, may each one of
us really believe that by way of the Throne we have unlimited
power.*

~ANNIE ARMSTRONG